The Open University

A219 Exploring the Classical World

Block 4
Rome – City and People

Valerie Hope and Janet Huskinson

This publication forms part of an Open University course A219 *Exploring the Classical World*. Details of this and other Open University courses can be obtained from the Student Registration and Enquiry Service, The Open University, PO Box 197, Milton Keynes, MK7 6BJ, United Kingdom: tel. +44 (0)870 333 4340, email general-enquiries@open.ac.uk

Alternatively, you may visit the Open University website at http://www.open.ac.uk where you can learn more about the wide range of courses and packs offered at all levels by The Open University.

To purchase a selection of Open University course materials visit http://www.ouw.co.uk, or contact Open University Worldwide, Michael Young Building, Walton Hall, Milton Keynes MK7 6AA, United Kingdom for a brochure. tel. +44 (0)1908 858785; fax +44 (0)1908 858787; email ouwenq@open.ac.uk

The Open University
Walton Hall, Milton Keynes
MK7 6AA

Edited and designed by The Open University.

Typeset by The Open University.

Printed in the United Kingdom by TJ International Ltd, Padstow.

ISBN 0 7492 9651 8

1.2

B/a219_b3_e1i2_0749296518

CONTENTS

Introduction to Block 4

Block timetable

This block comprises six weeks' work: that is, five study weeks and a final week to write TMA 05. Part 1 of the block should take approximately two weeks to study, Part 2 one week and Part 3 two weeks.

Aims and objectives

1   To acquire skills relevant to the study of the social history of Rome during the late republic and early empire.

2   To study critically a range of primary sources – literary, visual, archaeological and epigraphic – using an interdisciplinary method.

3   To gain an overview of the key issues and debates relevant to topics such as slavery, family life and mass entertainment in ancient Rome.

Materials required

To study this block you will need:

- Radice, B. (trans.) (1969) *The Letters of the Younger Pliny* (*PL*)

- Beard, M. and Crawford, M. (1999) *Rome in the Late Republic: Problems and Interpretations* (Beard and Crawford)

- *Oxford Companion to Classical Civilization* (*OCCC*)

- Book of Essays: *Experiencing the Classical World* (*ECW*)

- Readings Book 2

- Illustrations Book

- Audio-Visual Notes 2

- Assignment Book

- CD5, 'Satire in the city of Rome'

- DVD4, Section 1, 'Roman funerary monuments'; Section 2, 'Power and people'; Section 3, 'Roman baths'

- eDesktop ('ICT': timeline, pronunciation guide; 'Course links Block 4'

Introducing social history

The subject of this block is the social history of the city of Rome. It will build on your work in Block 3 where you studied the development of Rome and the politics and literary culture of the late republic and early empire. The emphasis in this block is on certain aspects of life in the city of Rome.

Before studying this material, let's pause to consider what is meant by social history, which can be difficult to define precisely or concisely. In seeking to do so we might think of some of the topics that it embraces, such as family life or living conditions, and equally some of the things that it is not expected to involve, such as politics, battles and economics. Social history is about people and how they interact; it is the study of society and social relationships in a given period.

The study of the social history of Rome has expanded greatly since the 1960s. The subject has been affected by broader academic trends, such as feminism, methods employed in researching history in other periods, and by theories promoted by disciplines such as anthropology and sociology. It's worth remembering that history, as a subject and a discipline, is always affected by the context in which it is studied, researched and taught. How we choose to study the Greeks and Romans in the twenty-first century says a lot about us, just as the way in which these same subjects were studied in the past has the potential to reveal a good deal about previous generations.

Roman social historians aim to understand how Roman society worked. Topics such as slavery, the family, demography, housing and living conditions have all been studied and continue to be illuminated by techniques employed by Roman social historians. However, it is worth remembering that the term 'social history' only serves as a convenient label. No part of the past can be neatly compartmentalised. Politics, economics, law and war have all impacted on how people lived and interacted, and there is no sharp dividing line between studying social history and political, economic, military or cultural history. I'm sure your study of the course so far could illustrate this point well. Modern scholars use labels to help them to categorise their studies, to suggest where the emphasis and focus of their particular approach lies. In using the term at the beginning of this block I'm indicating that we are going to take a specific approach to the ancient evidence, evidence that might in other contexts illustrate other points equally as well. We are going to ask questions about how people lived and then evaluate the extent to which the ancient sources yield appropriate evidence and answers.

So how can we study 'Roman social history'? Take a few moments to consider any potential difficulties or drawbacks (you do not need to make notes).

There is a mass of evidence that can be examined to illustrate aspects of Roman social history. Just about everything from laws to graffiti has the potential to tell us something about social relationships. Social history embraces interdisciplinary study, drawing on, for example, literature (in all its forms), archaeology, architecture, art and philosophy for clues and data. However, we must confront the limitations of the available evidence when viewed from the perspective of social history. Much of the human past, of whatever period, remains inaccessible to us and there is only so much we can understand and reconstruct. Someone writing a letter or carving a tombstone did not always include information that we would like to know two thousand years later.

We may wish, for example, to reconstruct a Roman funeral or the curriculum of a particular school, but the evidence may not be recorded. In any period people often fail to describe what to them is commonplace. And some types of evidence, which we have for later historical periods, are not available. To possess extensive census returns or large collections of birth, marriage and death certificates would alter considerably the reference points for the social historian of Rome, as would more personal and mundane items such as shopping lists, photograph albums and love letters. This is not to say that these things, or their equivalent, did not exist in the ancient world, but that they rarely survive in quantity. Instead, the social historian of the Roman period is forced to draw on diverse evidence in order to piece together a picture of aspects of Roman life. In addition, the evidence that is available needs to be evaluated with care, for the sources have certain inherent biases. Literary texts, for example, tend to reflect the voices of a wealthy male élite and thus finding the voices of women, slaves and children can be challenging. Other difficulties are created by space and time. The Roman empire was vast and long lived and across this spectrum attitudes, language, behaviour and expectations may not have been uniform. There may have been large social differences, say, between 120 BCE and CE 120, and between the city of Rome and the province of Spain. In short, there is no such thing as an average 'Roman'.

Many of these difficulties of interpretation are obvious, inevitable and not unique to the Roman period. In any society people have diverse experiences. Social history seeks to identify trends and patterns of any period, and some generalisations are inevitable. In studying Roman social history we have to be particularly aware of the limits of the evidence; to draw together varied types of sources with no concern for their original context in terms of genre, place, time and audience would be to create a composite picture with little validity.

You will need to keep these issues in mind as you explore some aspects of the social history of Rome in your work on this block. It has not been possible to include everything that might come under the umbrella of 'Roman social history', but the topics chosen should allow you to identify and explore central elements of life in Rome and discover the inherent difficulties of interpretation and reconstruction facing modern scholars. The block is divided into three parts. In Part 1 we will consider who lived in Rome and the significance of social and legal status. You will be introduced to *The Letters of the Younger Pliny* (set book) as a medium for exploring social relations and interactions in Rome of the late first and early second century CE, and explore topics such as slavery and dining. In Part 2 you will explore the role of the family in Roman life and the particular challenge of investigating the silent voice of the Roman child. Part 3 focuses on social interaction in public spaces – how people met in venues such as the theatre, amphitheatre and baths, and how behaviour at these venues defined both the people and the structures.

Part 1 The people of Rome

In this part of the block we will ask questions about who lived in the city of Rome, how people were differentiated and how various social groups interacted. Your work is divided into five sections focusing on the social order, the social world of Pliny the Younger, dining, slavery, and status at death. You will work with the set book – *The Letters of the Younger Pliny* – looking in particular at how Pliny defines his relations with others, including 'clients' (see Section 1.2) and ex-slaves. Slavery in the Roman world will also provide a link to the ancient philosophy of Stoicism and one of its important followers – Seneca the Younger. You will also be introduced to working with Roman epitaphs and funerary monuments. A key methodological issue that will emerge is the importance of evaluating the bias of status (especially the élite bias) present in the available sources.

1.1   The social order

A useful starting point in the study of a city and its population is to establish the number of its inhabitants. In the modern context, population size is often seen as one of the defining factors of a settlement. The number of inhabitants justifies claims to status as a village, town or city, and can be viewed as an index of economic growth or decline. Population statistics may also define the settlement in terms of demographic factors such as age, gender, wealth and ethnicity.

We do not possess comparable figures and statistics for the city of Rome. No ancient source tells us explicitly or exactly how many people lived there. Even when we are provided with numbers that may be relevant to population size – for example, the number of male citizens killed in a given battle – these need to be treated with caution. Many numbers recorded in ancient writings, be it battle casualties or the buildings in a city, often served a rhetorical purpose as the impression created by numbers was more important than accuracy. Nevertheless, modern scholars have attempted to estimate the ancient population size by extrapolating from various pieces of evidence, such as the number of citizens receiving the corn dole, the quantity of corn imports, the hectarage of the built-up areas of the city, and the number of residential buildings present in the fourth century CE. Comparisons have also been made with modern population densities. These estimates suggest a population in the late republic and early empire of around one million. However, none of these methods of calculation can claim to be exact. Furthermore, breaking down the suggested figure of one million into anything meaningful – knowing what proportion were men, women and children, young or old, slave or free – is even more problematic. Estimates of the size and relative proportions in that population are useful because they allow us to imagine aspects of life in the city, but they remain estimates. What we can evaluate with more certainty is what is known about the population in terms of its make-up or constituent elements, even if we cannot provide supporting numbers, proportions and percentages.

Exercise

Using your earlier reading in Block 3, Section 2.2 and Beard and Crawford (Chapter Four, 'Political Institutions', pp.40–49) as a starting point, write notes on the following:

1   Make a list of the different social groups present in Rome. If you find that there are any groups or terms that are new or unfamiliar to you, then find out a few basic details about these.

2   What impact, if any, did the change from republic to empire have on the social order?

You may also find the *OCCC* entry 'status, legal and social' useful. Broaden your search according to your needs by using *OCCC* and/or the internet.

Note: be realistic about how much time you spend on the first part of this exercise. You are only asked to provide a list; how much you wish to expand on this is a matter for your own judgement.

Discussion

1   Here are some of the groups that I identified. (Your list may be unlike mine or be organised differently, but I hope you identified at least some of the following.) You may have noted social groups based on wealth, power and privilege (or lack of it), such as senators and *equites*; or those distinguished by legal status, such as Roman citizens, slaves, freed slaves and non-citizen foreigners. In addition, you may have considered social groupings based on age, gender or occupation. Note that legal status was generally fixed – for example, you were either a citizen or you were not – whereas social status could be affected by many elements, some of which, such as wealth and occupation, were fluid. In reality, legal and social status combined and overlapped to create an individual's status profile. So there were varied ways in which the people of ancient Rome were grouped, and these groupings, however closely or loosely followed, helped to define how people

interacted. For many people status was multi-dimensional. The same man might be an ex-slave, a citizen, wealthy, of non-Roman extraction, elderly and a merchant.

If there are any terms about which you feel uncertain, such as *equites* or Roman citizen, then take this opportunity to consolidate your learning by looking them up in *OCCC*.

2   On one level the change in the political system from republic to empire had far-reaching effects on the social order. The impact on the senators and *equites* was substantial. Power was now concentrated in the hands of one man rather than 'shared' among the élite. Senatorial status and the value of its magistracies were undermined. However, the senatorial and equestrian orders continued to exist and were still important. The élite remained wealthy and privileged if not as powerful as before. For the other inhabitants of the city little may have changed. Certainly the significance of the citizens' votes declined as decision making was now dominated by the emperor, but then we can question how real citizen participation had been in the late republic (see Essay Six in *Experiencing the Classical World*). For the disenfranchised – slaves, women and children – changes in the power structures may have impacted little on their social and legal status.

I do not wish to underplay the changes afoot in Rome; they must have made an impression on everyone's lives. But when thinking purely in terms of the social structure of the city we may wish to question whether major political change had any impact. This is not to suggest that the social structure was chronologically static. In your reading you may have noted, for example, the decline of the patrician families, or the development of distinctions between *honestiores* and *humiliores* in the later empire. Some of these changes had political influences and/or repercussions. However, other elements of social and legal status remained largely unchanged in the years of the decline of the republic and the rise of the emperors.

I have highlighted this chronological element because, in the introduction to the block, we noted the importance of looking at evidence in context, one essential element of which is period. When we read a letter or a legal text, or look at a building, we need to consider the period in which it was made. For much of this block you will be looking at evidence that dates from the late republic through to the early second century CE. However, because evidence for some topics such as slavery and childhood is sparse, we will, when necessary, look beyond this period and thus you will need to be constantly aware of the chronology of the sources used. In addition you will be encouraged to think about some elements of chronological change: to what extent were things done, said or thought differently in, say, Cicero's day from that in Pliny's?

We have already noted that many aspects of social status were the same under the both the republic and empire. Let's now explore this further by thinking about the experiences of Cicero (106–43 BCE) and Pliny the Younger (CE 61–*c*.111).

Exercise

Read the *OCCC* entries for Cicero and Pliny the Younger and make some brief notes on their backgrounds, upbringing and public careers. Add some key dates from their lives to the timeline on your eDesktop. At this stage you need not dwell on the literary output of either man. Remember you have already looked at the *OCCC* entry for Cicero while working on Block 3; here it will be sufficient to focus on the first few pages of the entry and you may wish to reuse some of the notes you took in Block 3, Part 4.

What similarities and differences were there in the lives of Cicero and Pliny the Younger in terms of their public careers?

Discussion

Marcus Tullius Cicero was born in Arpinum in 106 BCE; Caius Plinius Caecilius Secundus (Pliny the Younger) was born in Comum in CE 61. Both men were from equestrian families, studied rhetoric and became advocates in the law courts of Rome. Both followed the *cursus honorum* (see Block 3, Part 2) which involved military service and the posts of quaestor, praetor and consul. Both spent time in the provinces – Cicero as proconsul of Cilicia and Pliny as an imperial legate in Bithynia-Pontus. So there are clear similarities in how the careers of these men progressed and in their roles as leading senators. There were differences, however, occasioned by the political backdrop against which their careers progressed. Cicero, as you know from your work on Block 3, was caught up in the competitive politics of his day which, among other things, caused him to spend some time in exile and ultimately led to his assassination. Pliny served under the emperors and some of the imperial administrative posts that he held reflect this, as does the nature of the legal cases in which he was involved. Governors might still be tried, but Pliny was hardly in a position to make speeches condemning political rivals. Pliny disliked the rule of the emperor Domitian, but did not articulate this until after the death of the latter when he fulsomely praised the emperor Trajan under whom he held the consulship.

The similarities and differences in the public careers of Cicero and Pliny reflect both the continuities and discontinuities between republic and empire. Nevertheless both men were senators and, in their day, men of importance.

In this block we will be looking at a range of evidence, but there will be frequent references to the letters of Pliny and to a lesser extent the works of Cicero, including his letters. The correspondence of Pliny will be explored for what it reveals about certain aspects of life in Rome. Central to this is Pliny's social circle and relationships – the people he writes to, those he defends in court, those whose interests he supports, his friends, his opponents, the emperor, his family, his slaves and his freedmen. At first glance this list appears to represent a wide range of people, but as your work progresses the narrowness of Pliny's circle and his perspectives on others will become apparent. The challenge is to fill the gaps. To what extent can we access other social groups or reconstruct attitudes and perspectives that differ from those of Pliny and his circle?

1.2   Pliny and patronage

Pliny the Younger wrote extensively in various differing genres. Most of this literary output has not survived,but what we do have, and thus what he is now most famous for, are his letters. The roles and purposes of letters are varied. In modern society – even in a high-tech age – letters perform many functions, both casual and formal. The same was probably true in the ancient context, although the accidents of survival can make it difficult to reconstruct the full versatility of the form. We do have some personal and informal correspondence, such as letters written on papyri found in Egypt and tablets from Britain (such as that shown in Figure 4.1) which preserve brief exchanges between family and acquaintances, and these were never intended for publication. However, letter writing was also a literary genre and most surviving letters from the ancient period represent the output of the educated élite, many of whom wrote with the intention of publishing their correspondence.

It is striking that the *OCCC* contains no entry for 'letters' or 'letter writing'. Most other literary genres appear to be represented – epic, elegiac poetry, epigrams, lyric and satire all have entries. The much larger volume from which the *OCCC* is derived, the *Oxford Classical Dictionary*, does contain an entry under letters. Clearly the *OCCC* cannot contain everything, nor can we know the basis for all editorial decisions, but it may be the case that the entry on letters was excluded because letter writing was less well

Figure 4.1 A birthday invitation from Claudia Severa to Sulpicia Lepidina. Writing tablet from Vindolanda, 2.23cm x 9.6cm. The British Museum, London, inv. P&EE 1986 101,64. © The Trustees of the British Museum.

acknowledged by the ancients and less well developed than other literary genres. Cicero noted that there were different types of letters (Cicero, *Letters to His Friends* 2.4) and his own correspondence provided a model for subsequently published collections of them. However, it remains unclear how much of his correspondence Cicero intended to be published, because much of it appears to have been collected and edited after his death. Subsequent authors were more conscious of writing for public consumption and other genres also adopted and adapted the letter format. The letter form was employed by poets such as Ovid and Horace, and also used in philosophical discussions. You will encounter the 'moral letters' of Seneca the Younger later in this block.

The letters of Pliny the Younger were undoubtedly influenced by those of Cicero. Pliny admired Cicero's oratorical skills and works and wished to model his literary career on that of the champion of the republic (Pliny, *Letters* 4.8). His letters were written with publication very much in mind and Pliny edited them to create a well-considered portrait of himself and his life.

For an overview of his literary output and technique you should refer to the *OCCC* entry on Pliny and read this in full now if you have not already done so. I would also suggest that you read *Letter* 1.1 to access Pliny's stated intentions. The 'Introduction' to *The Letters of the Younger Pliny* contains more information on his life, career and the subject matter of his letters. It is not essential that you read this now, but you will find it beneficial to do so at some stage during your work on this block.

The issue of genre is highly relevant to the context and evaluation of Pliny's letters as a source, especially for the social historian. As we've seen, Pliny was a leading politician of his day but, unlike Cicero, he was not writing under a republican form of government (albeit a dying one), but under a political regime in which he was required to exercise tact, especially in works that were openly intended for public consumption. The letters are not overtly political, but they are set against Pliny's life in court and politics. In terms of content Pliny's letters touch on social interaction and allow a pseudo-dialogue of considered observations on how one should behave. What Pliny says cannot be isolated from who he was and what and how he chose to write.

Pliny's letters evoke life in the Rome of his day and can be used in the study of topics such as social structure, family life, slavery, patronage and housing – subjects we will study in this block. Initially let's get to know Pliny and the nature of his letters by focusing on his friends and friendships.

Exercise

Read *Letter* 1.9

What does this letter suggest about Pliny's daily routine?

Discussion

This letter is carefully constructed to balance and contrast the descriptions of city and country life. The busy life of Rome stands in opposition to the relaxed life of the country villa. This contrast between business (*negotium*) and leisure (*otium*) is a common theme in Pliny's letters and here it is used to suggest that he lives a kind of double life. While in Rome Pliny is constantly busy attending social events such as weddings or supporting his friends; at his country estates he can relax and indulge in what is really important – reading and exercising the intellect. Pliny portrays his time in Rome as repetitive and trivial (note the reference to gossip). Certainly the events he describes do not suggest hard work, but are akin to what we might describe as 'networking'.

The letter should not be taken as a literal listing of what Pliny did and liked to do. It is a literary piece, an artistic play on the town and country contrast. How Pliny portrays himself is part of his image projection; his indulgence in the rural idyll and his literary pursuits are part of his élite status. However, the letter does indicate some elements of life in Rome for people of Pliny's social standing. We should note the importance to them of social contacts, of assisting people and of being seen at social events. Pliny's letter implies that his network of friends and acquaintances was important to him. Pliny may have derived emotional support from his friends, and in his letters he often records and thus shares their hopes and losses, but he also had other financial and political friendships. Pliny acted as a patron; he helped his friends and expected help in return.

Exercise

Look up 'patronage (non-literary)' in the *OCCC*.

What types of patronage operated in ancient Rome?

Discussion

The *OCCC* entry explores the terms 'patron' and 'client' and identifies three main areas in which they might be employed:

1   **Patrons of communities**. The towns and cities of the empire could use powerful individuals to promote and protect their interests in Rome.

2   **Ex-masters and ex-slaves**. On granting a slave freedom, the master became a patron and his freed slave a client who was bound to him by certain ties and obligations.

3   **Between citizens**. Lesser citizens might be tied to those more powerful and wealthy. In this reciprocal arrangement the powerful gained a supportive entourage and the poor financial support and someone to promote their interests.

The last category is the most difficult to define precisely. This type of patronage could pervade all aspects of society – it was not just a relationship between rich and poor. Senators might look to other senators – more influential than themselves – for help and support. The terms 'patron' and 'client' might not always be employed because the latter term, with its servile connotations, could be seen as insulting. But one's 'friends' might not all be on a level social footing and were expected to be supportive in any way they could. Note, in particular, the final paragraph of the *OCCC* entry and the importance ascribed to 'the general phenomenon of patronage'. It offered a sort of brockerage and contributed to social stability in the Roman world.

These three elements of patronage are all represented in Pliny's letters. Pliny acted as a patron of communities (see *Letter* 4.1, for example). In Section 1.4 we will consider Pliny and his relationship as patron with his freed slaves, but here we will look at how Pliny helped his personal friends.

Exercise

Read Pliny *Letters* 1.19, 2.9, 2.13 and 10.4. For interest you may also wish to read Cicero's letter to Lentulus Spinther (24)[1], in Reading 4.1.

1   How does Pliny characterise his friends?

2   What types of things does he do for them?

Discussion

1   The people Pliny promotes in these letters are male friends, some from childhood and from his home town. They could be seen as Pliny's social inferiors – they do not seem so wealthy or as well connected. However, these are still men of merit and standing in their own right. Pliny seems genuinely fond of them and he is upbeat and positive about their qualities. But in this context Pliny would hardly be negative because in writing these letters Pliny is 'selling' the merits of his friends to others. In supporting them he is to some degree putting his own reputation on the line, as he suggests in particular in *Letter* 2.9. The people that Pliny writes to in *Letters* 2.9 and 2.13 are his 'friends', but ones who are in a position to help his other friends and thus Pliny himself. Pliny is concerned about how he will be judged by his friends, and hence his anxiety in *Letter* 2.9 about the emperor's opinion. Note the tone of the letter written to the emperor (*Letter* 10.4): Pliny addresses the emperor, the ultimate patron, in a deferential style.

2   Pliny gives his friends money, he seeks electoral support for them, tries to gain them public offices and even promotion to the senate. He uses his powerful connections – including the emperor – to gain support and prestige for his friends, and to advance their public careers.

These are letters of recommendation, a sub-genre of the genre of letter writing. In such letters Pliny (and Cicero) would be expected to use particular phrases and present the case in a certain way. Pliny is not explicit about the benefit he receives for promoting these men, although he does mention the debts inherent in friendship. In these letters Pliny is pleading for others, not for himself; he is playing the role of patron. But by asking favours from others Pliny also becomes a 'client' and assumes that his 'friends' will do similar favours for him. This emphasises the reciprocal

---

[1] Note that this number in brackets relates to the numbering system in the Penguin edition of *Cicero: Selected Letters* (1982).

nature of the system; people exchanged favours and became indebted to each other. Personal contacts and recommendations were powerful and all important; personal ability and ambition may have been significant, but so was who you knew. With the help of these supportive networks people were able to advance socially, politically and financially.

In the city of Rome status mattered, but only a minority occupied the higher orders, and only a few could aspire to senatorial status or even the wealth of an *eques*. The patronage system pervaded society and could highlight the extremes of inequality. For the poor, playing the role of client may have been less about social advancement and more about simple survival. To be a client could involve a degree of humiliation – this is not revealed by Pliny, but is satirised by other contemporary writers.

Exercise

Read Martial, *Epigrams* 5.22 and 6.88, in Reading 4.2.

RB

What sort of relationship does Martial have with his patron?

Note: you will encounter Martial again later in this block when you will consider genre, technique and so forth. At this stage, simply record your initial response to these particular epigrams.

Discussion

Here there is a greater sense of inequality between patron and client. Martial constructs a picture in which he is doing all the work to maintain the relationship. It is Martial who has to cross the city to see his patron, only to find that he's gone out. It is Martial who has to watch what he says to his patron or suffer a financial penalty. Clearly, Martial must not forget his place.

Martial is writing satirically. There is an element of exaggeration and stereotyping in the portraits of patron and client that he paints. But he does provide a different perspective from that of Pliny – that of the financially unequal and somewhat downtrodden 'friend'. This shows that to build up a picture of social relationships and interactions in Rome we cannot look at Pliny alone, but as social historians we need to bring together different genres, authors and voices.

In addition to suggesting the importance of patronage for getting on and surviving, the works of Pliny and Martial also convey aspects of social etiquette: the importance of addressing people properly, of asking for favours in the correct way, and of knowing who you could use as an intermediary. In other words, in their society it was important to evaluate where you stood in relation to others; you needed to 'read' or recognise the status of others while simultaneously displaying your own rank or standing. People sought to differentiate themselves from others – the citizen from the freedman, the well-to-do from the poor. Status symbols were important, but people could use these incorrectly and be criticised or mocked by others. The next section explores how this could operate in one particular social setting – the dinner party.

1.3   The etiquette of dining

If we are what we eat, what do the dining habits of the Romans tell us about them? The *cena* was the biggest meal of the day and was consumed after the day's work. For most people, most days, the *cena* must have been mundane and ordinary, but dining did have the potential to become an important social activity. How often this was the case depended inevitably on who you were and the circles you moved in. To what extent was having a few friends (or indeed a crowd) round for dinner an opportunity to display and celebrate status distinctions?

The popular view of a Roman is one characterised by his relationship with food. The fat man reclining in an opulent setting, with a vast banquet before him while being fed and waited on by many slaves is an image frequently projected in films and popular fiction (Figure 4.2). This stereotype inevitably masks the diversity of Roman society, but is hardly surprising considering the élite bias of the available sources and some ancient descriptions of banqueting excesses (see, in particular, Martial, *Epigram* 3.82, and Petronius, *Satyricon* 26–73 in Readings Book 2). Can we challenge this stereotype? And was it challenged in antiquity? In this section we will evaluate some ancient views on dining and ask questions about what was and what was not socially acceptable behaviour.

Exercise

Read Pliny, *Letter* 2.6.

What does this letter suggest about gradations of status and how people were treated at dinner?

Discussion

Not everyone is treated equally at this dinner party. The host grades his friends and distinguishes the freed slaves. A social hierarchy – created by the host, but partly reflecting that present in wider society – is reinforced at the dining table. People are fed and watered according

Figure 4.2   Wall painting showing a banqueting scene, Pompeii.
Museo Nazionale, Naples, inv. 120092. Courtesy of the Ministero
per i Beni e le Attività Culturali. Guests recline and sit on couches
while attended by slaves in the foreground. To the left, a guest has
his shoes removed by a slave, and on the right, another slave assists a
bent figure who may be vomiting.

to their place in the social structure. Pliny does not approve and seems
to view such behaviour as a breach of etiquette, but this does not
mean that he thinks that everyone is equal. Pliny does not dispute the
existence of social distinctions, but considers that their display is not
always appropriate, unlike acting with a show of humility. Thus, at the
dinner table people should be 'fellow-diners'.

Pliny uses the letter to make a moral point about extravagance and
meanness, since in his view the host was too stingy to serve everyone the
best-quality food and wine, but his letter is also indicative of social habits
and shows that the social pecking order could be enforced on such
occasions. Dining and the dining habits of ancient Rome were an
important social activity. Pliny may not have approved fully, but he was
very aware that the evening's entertainment could say a lot about the host

and his guests. How you dined and with whom reflected your social status; giving and receiving dinner invitations was an aspect of the patronage system. As we saw in the previous section, people could be defined by their friends and friendships, and the *cena* was an opportunity both to celebrate and display existing bonds and to forge new ones. Note how Pliny describes himself 'as no particular friend' of the man he criticises, although he had still accepted the dinner invitation. The dinner table became a common literary theme, exploited in a continuing discussion of social conventions of what constituted good and bad behaviour, extravagance and modesty, pleasure and abstinence.

Did people agree with Pliny, or behave like the host he criticises? To investigate this we need to look at other sources and genres.

Exercise

Listen to the discussion on satirical writings as a source on CD5, 'Satire in the city of Rome'. Refer to Audio-Visual Notes 2 for help and further information.

Then, having listened to the audio discussion, read the following sources in Readings Book 2:

- Martial, *Epigrams* 2.37, 5.47, 7.20, 10.49 and 12.82, in Reading 4.2.

- Petronius, *Satyricon* 31–36, 40 and 49, in Reading 4.3. (You may, if you wish, read all of the extract from the *Satyricon*, but I suggest you focus on the chapters noted here.)

- Juvenal, *Satire* 5, in Reading 4.4. (You can read all of the *Satire*, but I suggest you focus on these sections 'Get one thing clear from the start ... will he send to a friend with heartburn' and '"Was it for this" you wail ... they won't come anywhere near you' and 'What farce or pantomime could be a bigger joke ... such a friend').

How is dining characterised here? Are any of the authors critical of the behaviour of those present?

Discussion

The material suggests the importance of dinner parties for negotiating status roles and displaying status symbols. In one respect these dinners were private events – they were held at home and the host controlled who attended. But simultaneously the host expected a reaction and possibly public comment from those present. (The issue of public versus private will be discussed in Part 3.) Who you invited, how you treated them in terms of the food, wine and entertainment you provided were all part of how you wished to portray yourself, evaluate your guests and celebrate (or not) your relationships. Taken to its extreme, dinner was a theatrical event, full of novelties and spectacle, an extravagant show designed to impress. The dinner could reflect the wider social order – the axis of power between free and slave, rich and poor, patron and client, could all be emphasised in how people were treated. In Juvenal's satire the food is graded and the poor client gets little of note; there is also a reference to the quality of the wine served at Trimalchio's feast (Petronius, *Satyricon* 34), and both Martial and Juvenal are critical of the hosts for their double standards and for insulting their guests. But they are critical of the guests too: those who fish for invitations, those who are greedy, and those who are prepared to humiliate themselves for such poor food. We need to be aware of genre here; these works are satires and epigrams, composed to make a point rather than to reflect accurately social realities. The tone of them is mildly comical and tongue-in-cheek, and the deliberate exaggeration or polarising of behaviour to create social stereotypes is a standard technique of these genres. Nevertheless, all this hints at underlying realities – people's insecurities and self awareness of personal status and the opinions of others.

Pliny was a man of high status, a member of the senatorial order, and his social circle reflected this. From his position of privilege he could look at others and perhaps be critical of their attempts to ape their betters, to create and reinforce social distinctions among their guests with the intention of making themselves look more important. It was perhaps easy to pretend to be humble (as Pliny advocates) when everyone knew you and the extent of your status and influence. Nor should we be fooled by Petronius, Martial and Juvenal speaking as if they were ordinary 'men in the street'. These authors were members of élite literary circles. They wrote largely for the entertainment of the élite, and may have been paid by them. For such authors, the poor client and the nouveau riche were particularly easy targets.

There are different ways of interpreting and reading these sources. If we read them literally, they suggest that extravagance was rife, that opulent dinner parties were all the rage, and that the modern stereotype of over-indulged Roman hosts and guests is well deserved. But the sources also imply that, although this sort of activity might occur, it was not necessarily the norm and was certainly not approved of by all. Thus we have evidence that the stereotype was, in fact, a Roman – not a modern – invention.

There was, then, a dialogue in élite literary genres about what was acceptable behaviour at the dinner table. This in itself suggests that dining was an important forum for the negotiation of status and identity. People reacted to what they ate, drank, saw and experienced, and dining was about more than simply food and drink (Figure 4.3), since it was also about how the host and his guests acted and interacted. People that broke the rules of accepted etiquette might be ridiculed by those that regarded themselves as socially superior. But would Trimalchio, the fictional ex-slave, have cared what people thought of him?

Figure 4.3   Wall painting of food, first century CE, from a *triclinium* in the property of Julia Felix, Pompeii, height 74cm. Museo Nazionale, Naples, inv. 8611. Courtesy of the Ministero per i Beni e le Attività Culturali. The glass bowl holds apples, grapes, pomegranates and figs. A pottery vessel holds dried fruit and leaning against this is a small amphora. The damaged left panel depicts further vessels and a cockerel.

In terms of social history, literary accounts of Roman dinner parties provide important insights into the existing social structure and how it operated, and I have chosen to focus on that here. But there are many other relevant issues and questions that may have struck you. For example, where and how did people sit when dining? Where was the dining room situated and how was it decorated? What was a humble *cena* like? What was it like to wait at table? What did slaves eat? We may not always be able to answer these questions fully, but asking the questions helps us to shape our knowledge of the Roman world and forces us to explore the available evidence in new ways. Thus, if we wanted to look further at dining in its social context we would need to investigate topics such as diet (for all social groups), food production, tableware and dining-room décor, and employ a wide and various range of sources.

1.4   Slave and free

A fundamental feature of Roman social structure was that everyone was either a slave or free. Roman society, at least within Rome and Italy, was a slave society in which the major source of labour was provided by men and women who were deprived of their freedom. Slaves were the tools and possessions of masters who had the power of life or death over them. Slaves could not own property, nor establish legitimate marriages, and any children born to slaves automatically became the property of the master.

If you have not already done so you should now read the *OCCC* entry on 'Slavery – Roman', written by Keith Bradley who has researched and written extensively on Roman slavery (Bradley, 1987; 1994). The entry serves as a useful introduction to slavery in the Roman world and covers elements such as the extent of slavery, the supply of slaves, slave employment and slave resistance – subjects that it will not be possible to explore fully here. You should note that slavery was not necessarily a lifelong state. Slaves could be freed and cross the divide into the free population. However, certain social stigmas would remain, as well as ties of obligation to the former master, which marked out the freed slave. Look up the *OCCC* entry on 'freedmen/freedwomen' if you wish to know more.

Returning to Bradley's *OCCC* entry, note the pivotal sentence: 'Practically all knowledge of classical slavery derives from sources representing the attitudes and ideology of slave-owners' (p.672). In other words we rarely glimpse the slave's perspective. We may know what a master thought of his slaves, but not what the slave thought of him. Is there any way round this? Can we ever reconstruct a slave's attitude? Bradley suggests one possibility: by comparing Rome and 'New World slave societies'. Inferences from more recent slave-owning societies yield some evidence from the slaves' perspective and suggest the possibility of strategies of 'accommodation and resistance'. Bradley considers where we may find evidence for this in the existing sources for the Roman period, by looking at evidence of slaves being obedient and loyal, running away or even openly revolting (Figure 4.4). Bradley's summary provides a good example of social history in action; Roman slaves have left us little direct evidence, but we can piece together some aspects of their experiences and thus partially reinstate their voice.

In this section we are going to employ similar principles to explore some aspects of the attitudes and ideology of the slave owners. As Bradley has signalled, this should be more straightforward than reconstructing the slaves' experiences since most of the sources reflect the masters' perspectives. We will focus on two masters, Pliny and Seneca the Younger. How did they treat their slaves? How did they expect other masters to treat slaves?

Figure 4.4   An iron collar with bronze slave tag, diameter 12cm. Museo Nazionale, Rome (Terme di Diocleziano). © 2003, Photo SCALA, Florence – courtesy of the Ministero per i Beni e le Attività Culturali. The tag offers a reward of a gold coin on the return of the wearer to his master Zoninus.

Pliny was very conscious of how he presented himself as a master of slaves and as a patron of freed slaves.

Exercise

Read Pliny, *Letters* 5.19 and 8.16. For comparison you may wish to read Cicero's *Letter to his family* (57)[2] in Reading 4.1. (Tiro was a freed slave.)

How do these letters characterise Pliny as a master (and patron)? Do they allow us insight into the perspectives of the slaves and ex-slaves?

[2] See note 1.

Discussion

In *Letter* 5.19 we see Pliny using his network of friends once more. He wishes to send his freed slave Zosimus on a recuperative trip to a friend's villa in the south of France. Pliny justifies his request by praising Zosimus in a similar manner to his other recommendations. However, Zosimus is no man of note about to embark on a public career, but an actor and entertainer. Pliny seems genuinely fond of him, but his letter emphasises his own kindness, suffering and concern. Pliny acts in Zosimus' interests but does not address Zosimus' pain or preferences. Similarly, in *Letter* 8.16, the subject matter may be illness among Pliny's slaves, but the objective is to define a good master. Pliny is a good master because he is generous, kind and humane, and he contrasts his behaviour with the inhumanity of those who see slaves as a purely financial investment. Once more we do not have the slaves' perspectives, although the subtext is that the slaves should be grateful to have such a master. The letter is not concerned with the pain and suffering of the slaves, or with how they deal with their bereavements; instead it is Pliny's grief that takes centre stage.

Pliny's letters are carefully written to reveal how he wishes to be seen and judged. A modern reader may be a little cynical about his protestations and note that his concern is for himself first and his slaves second. Nevertheless, Pliny thought of himself as a good master and, in comparison to some others, he probably had good reason to regard himself as such. Pliny was not alone in what he advocated for an element of humanity was expected behaviour from the élite. Pliny was influenced by ancient philosophy, especially Stoicism, which promoted principles by which people could live their lives well. One of the great Stoic philosophers and writers of the Roman period was Seneca the Younger.

Exercise

Please read the following:

- an extract from Seneca, *Letter* 47 in Reading 4.5, from the beginning to the end of the fifth paragraph.

- Essay Seven, 'Seneca: a philosophy of living' by Carolyn Price, in *Experiencing the Classical World*.

You may wish to add some key dates to the timeline on the eDesktop about Seneca and his career.

As you read:

1   make some notes on Seneca, his life, career and writings. Focus in particular on his status and his use of the genre of letter writing;

2   evaluate Seneca's attitude to slavery.

Note: I will be referring to Essay Seven later. At this stage you should read the whole essay, but focus in particular on the sections that address Seneca's life and attitudes to slavery.

Discussion

1   Seneca was born in Spain in 4 BCE to an equestrian family, but pursued a senatorial career and became a leading figure in Rome, especially during the reign of Nero. He was forced to commit suicide in CE 65. Seneca wrote extensively, promoting his beliefs in Stoic philosophy. It is worth noting that he was writing before Pliny the Younger, and that, like Pliny, his letters were written with publication in mind. The letters are addressed to Lucilius, an adherent of Epicurean philosophy, and explore a range of topics from a philosophical standpoint. This reveals the versatility of the genre of letter writing, because the subject matter is very different from that in most of Pliny's letters. Seneca uses the medium to discuss issues of importance to him in a 'friendly, personal tone' (*Experiencing the Classical World*, p.154), but his letters resemble themed essays rather than informal correspondence between friends.

2   Seneca suggests that slave owners should live on good terms with their slaves. Slaves are human beings and deserve to be treated as such. Slaves may even be better and wiser people than their owners since they are only slaves by chance. Seneca contrasts his ideals with how people behave. Many masters are so obsessed with luxury and display that their slaves become little more than tools for the furtherance of this. In reading the description of dinner-time extravagances and the role of slaves in these you may have recalled aspects of your work in Section 1.3. (For the views of Trimalchio – a fictional ex-slave – on slavery see Petronius, *Satyricon* 71 in Reading 4.3.)

Seneca's letter provides some insights into slavery and some of the humiliations that a slave might have to endure, but the real focus of the letter is on the behaviour of slave masters. Both Seneca and Pliny polarise masters as good or bad; they create stereotypes from which it is difficult to isolate the reality. As with the comments on dining etiquette that we encountered earlier, these sources suggest that not everyone lived up to the élite's (or élite's philosophical) ideal of good and acceptable behaviour. In addition, these letters only address some aspects of the slave–master relationship and only some types of slavery. Those slaves who formed part of the household, who were for the most part domestic town dwellers, probably fared considerably better than many of their counterparts. We learn very little from any literary source about rural slaves, those working in the mines or on chain gangs. These slaves probably had little direct contact with their masters, but were cruelly exploited by them. The general silence of the masters of non-domestic slaves is probably telling in itself. Many masters may have viewed these slaves as little more than an economic asset, thus creating, from our perspective, an unfortunate meeting of social and economic history.

Seneca and Pliny may have viewed themselves as good masters (at least towards their household slaves) but neither challenges the institution of slavery. They do not view slavery itself as unjust, nor do they condemn the real physical and mental deprivations of slaves. Instead, they focus on the inherent moral dangers for the master.

Although Pliny accepted slavery and saw himself as a good master, there may have been limits to his tolerance.

Exercise

Read Pliny, *Letter* 3.14.

1   What sort of master was Macedo?

2   What is Pliny's attitude towards the slaves involved?

Discussion

1   Macedo is the opposite of what Pliny idealises elsewhere. According to Pliny he is a cruel master and deservedly unpopular with his slaves. Note Pliny's reference to his background: his father had allegedly been a slave and Pliny interprets this as potential problem in the snobbish world of Rome. He implies that Macedo wished to distance himself from his past and thus treated his slaves particularly badly.

2   On one level Pliny has some sympathy for the slaves. The master was cruel and got what he deserved. But the final part of the first paragraph is revealing. Pliny implies that slaves are brutal and

can act without reason. To be a kind and considerate master like Pliny is not adequate protection. The façade of kind masters and contented slaves could easily break.

Masters might fear their slaves – after all, many masters were surrounded and outnumbered by slaves – and this might lead them to be distant and even cruel. Despite the protestations of Seneca and Pliny, there could be limits to humanity.

How you treated your slaves, like how you dined, could say a lot about you. The ideal was that the élite master should be a humane master. But it is difficult to go beyond the idealised veneer of humanity depicted in the literary sources, or the counter stereotype of cruelty sometimes portrayed. To attempt this we would, like Bradley, need to construct an investigative framework drawing on a wider range of evidence. It is relatively easy for us to hear the voices of Pliny or Seneca and those in stark opposition to them, but the reality for many masters and slaves lay probably somewhere in between. Without the voice of the slave our perspective is decidedly one-sided.

1.5   Tombstones and status

As a result of their social position slaves have left us no literary accounts of their experiences, for they were denied a direct voice in literature. So far in Part 1 we have focused on literary sources, mainly letters, satirical writing and philosophy. In looking at these as evidence for topics such as patronage, dining and slavery we have been struck by both their evocative nature but also their biases. Literature was the product of the élite; it was not written by the poor client or the exploited slave. Is there any way we can redress the balance? Is there evidence that can provide a different perspective? One important source is funerary and sepulchral inscriptions. These name people other than the élite and sometimes provide biographical details. What is more, these simple texts were frequently composed and commissioned by the free poor, slaves and freed slaves. Epitaphs are a fascinating source for information on all social groups in Rome, especially those who are rarely accessed by other means.

You have already worked with some epitaphs. Look back to Block 3, Section 3.2 and the inscriptions found in the tomb of the Scipios. You will find some more examples of epitaphs in Reading 4.8.

Exercise

Read the following epitaphs in Reading 4.8:

(a)   *CIL* VI 1274 (Caecilia Metella)

(b)   *CIL* VI 1013/1014 (Eurysaces)

(c)   *CIL* VI 2246 (Rabirii)

(d)   *CIL* VI 6327 (Gemellus)

(e)   *Année Epigraphique* 1955, 24 (Publius Sulpicius Peregrinus)

(f)   *CIL* VI 16631 (Minicia Marcella)

The Latin text is supplied for some of the epitaphs for reference purposes, so that you can gain an impression of the original appearance of the inscriptions and some of the conventions employed. You are not expected to be able to read or translate Latin for this course.

Look at the Latin and then at the English translation. What difference strikes you? It is something you can note without reading either.

Discussion

You were probably struck by the relative difference in length between the Latin and the English translation. This is because the Latin is full of abbreviations – single letters or small groups of letters stand for whole words: so, for example, the letter C for Caius or F for filius/filia (son/daughter). Reading Latin inscriptions can be a bit like cracking a code. From a practical point of view the use of abbreviations saved money. Cutting stone may have been expensive so it made sense to reduce the number of letters involved. However, the abbreviations are also suggestive of how these texts functioned. Epitaphs were often standardised and formulaic – saying the same things in similar ways. Thus even for the semi-literate it may have been relatively easy to decipher the basic content of the epitaph because groups of letters acted as symbols. Compare them, for example, with the letters RIP (Rest in Peace), sometimes inscribed on modern British tombstones.

Exercise

Can you identify the names in the epitaphs? Who is named?

Discussion

Names are an essential part of the epitaph. After all, epitaphs are about people – and it is through a name that the deceased is both identified and remembered. In addition, Latin epitaphs frequently named a commemorator: that is to say, those who set up the memorial recorded their name as well, and often their relationship to the deceased. So the father of Publius Sulpicius Peregrinus is also named in the epitaph he composed for his son. In some epitaphs commemorator and commemorated are the same person because people could choose to set up their own memorial before death. This was probably the case with the tomb of Eurysaces.

Exercise

What differences do you notice in the names found in different epitaphs?

Discussion

The names differ in length and in whether they incorporate details such as the father's name and voting tribe. Look back to Block 3, Section 3.4 which looks at names and explores their constituent elements. The main point to note here is that the names provide clues about people's social status and allow us to identify citizens, slaves and freed slaves. The names here suggest that Caecilia Metella, Publius Sulpicius Peregrinus and Minicia Marcella are freeborn citizens. The L for 'libertus' in the name of Caius Rabirius Hermodorus indicates that he is a freed slave. The single name of Gemellus suggests that he is a slave. Marcus Vergilius Eurysaces, Rabiria Demaris and Usia Prima are not specifically identified as freeborn citizens or freed slaves. Epitaphs could reveal legal status, but there was no necessity or obligation to do so.

Exercise

In addition to the names, what other information is provided in the epitaphs?

Discussion

We've already noted the presence of statements of relationship between the commemorated person and the commemorator(s). Epitaphs might also include an age at death and a reference to the job of the deceased. In our examples, the age at death is provided for Publius Sulpicius Peregrinus and Minicia Marcella. Note how the age statement for the latter is abbreviated but still detailed (V(ixit) A(nnis) XII M(ensibus) XI D(iebus) VII). Jobs are given for Marcus Vergilius Eurysaces, Publius Sulpicius Peregrinus and Gemellus. Usia Prima has a religious role associated with her name, which gives her prestige. Some epitaphs might contain additional information – a career biography, eulogy or poem. For examples, look back to the Scipio epitaphs studied in Block 3, Section 3.2. But most epitaphs were short and focused on the names of the deceased and the bereaved. Notably they do not include a date – something that we take for granted in a modern epitaph.

Exercise

How would you evaluate the epitaphs as a source for the social historian?

Discussion

The epitaphs name people of different social groups and allow some insights into their world and relationships. The very fact that people such as slaves had epitaphs is interesting, as is how different groups are characterised. For example, contrast the style of the Scipio epitaphs with that of the slave childminder Gemellus. However, many epitaphs are limited in what they reveal and are also formulaic and standardised. Are epitaphs a product of convention rather than of genuine grief? Do people tell the truth in them – is it acceptable to speak ill of the dead? There are also other things that would aid our evaluation. From what period do they date? Where were they found? What type of monument were they found on? Who would have seen and read these epitaphs? Some of these questions are answered for you in the brief description that precedes each epitaph and you will see most of these epitaphs when you watch DVD4, Section 1, 'Roman funerary monuments'. However, you should note that epitaphs can be difficult to date exactly and that many have been removed from their original context.

It has been estimated that 100,000 inscriptions survive from the city of Rome and that as many as 75 per cent of these are epitaphs (Bodel, 2001, pp.8, 30). They thus provide an access point to the population at large and attempts have been made to use this evidence to create statistics concerning social groups, age at death and family structure (see Part 2). However, epigraphic evidence has its limitations. The surviving epitaphs must still represent only a small percentage of the people who lived in Rome. If the population of Rome is taken to be one million, it can be estimated that more than 30,000 people died per annum (Bodel, 2000, pp.128–9). Many epitaphs and tombstones have probably not survived, and we also need to be aware that many deaths were not marked in this way. Not everyone could have afforded or wished to have their grave indicated in this fashion. Epitaphs may have appealed to some social groups more than others and their popularity may have varied across time. We must also bear in mind that when we speak of epitaphs we are decontextualising them, removing them from the tomb or tombstone with which they were originally associated. In evaluating epitaphs we need to be aware that the original environment would have dictated how they were read and understood.

Many of these potential problems are reflected in attempts to use statements of age recorded in epitaphs to create statistical data on age at death. Many epitaphs record the age at which the commemorated person died. It might be thought that if we took these dates we could use them to explore the age profile of the Roman population and establish an average age at death. However, close analysis soon reveals some difficulties. Not all epitaphs contain age statements and those that do may not record age accurately – there was a tendency in the ancient world to round numbers up or down. Equally the inclusion of age statements appears to have defined certain groups, especially boys, which reflects the higher social esteem attached to males and the dashed hopes of parents who lost their sons. In other words, any statistics derived from this data are skewed by the circumstances of their production.

So there was a culture of commemoration in existence in Rome in which not everyone could or wanted to participate equally. We can explore this by looking at some of the monuments that survive and by considering who set them up and why. Funerary monuments were a communicative medium that could be used carefully to construct an identity for the deceased and his or her survivors.

 You should now watch DVD4, Section 1, 'Roman funerary monuments' and refer to Audio-Visual Notes 2. The last two tracks of this section are relevant to Part 2 of this block; you may wish to watch these now, but will need to do so again later.

Social status, wealth, age and occupation were all part of how an individual was defined and this could be highlighted in funerary monuments. However, we need to be wary of making simple analogies. The biggest tombs were not always associated with the élite. The cemetery did not present a simple visual parallel to the social order but a medium for the negotiation of social identity. We saw in the DVD that many elaborate tombs were associated with freed slaves. This was a group that had conflicting aspects to their identity. Their background was a stigma, and therefore they would always be servile. Yet ex-slaves were citizens and the parents of future citizen children, and a few became extremely wealthy. In life the freed slave faced social difficulties, but in death he could be buried and remembered as a success. Funerary monuments may have gained a special significance for this group.

Exercise

Read Petronius, *Satyricon* 71 in Reading 4.3.

RB

What are the central elements of Trimalchio's tomb?

Discussion

Trimalchio's tomb pulls out all the stops! Trimalchio wants the tomb to appeal to the passer-by by being large, grand and elaborately decorated. It is to be a visual feast of images. There are to be statues, reliefs of gladiators fighting and ships sailing as well as images of Trimalchio being generous to others. The tomb will contain a clock (a sundial) to attract people's attention and encourage them to read Trimalchio's name and epitaph. Trimalchio wants the tomb to reflect his identity, and the design highlights what he regarded as some of the important elements of his life – such as the office he held, his generosity and his family. Others may have viewed his life differently. Trimalchio wants to be remembered and he is aware that memory can be fickle, as can respect for the dead. Hence the need for a guard!

Trimalchio is a fictional creation – a grossly exaggerated character, a stereotype taken to extreme for comical impact. However, surviving tombs to freed slaves from Rome and elsewhere in the empire suggest that there is some basis for this characterisation (Figures 4.5, 4.6 and 4.7). The tombs of well-to-do freed slaves are fascinating and provide a contrast to the picture we have from literary evidence. In literature, the freed slaves may be the butt of jokes, but in the real, non-literary, world they could clearly make and leave their mark. Epitaphs and tombs suggest a wider picture of society, giving expression to how prosperous freed slaves wished to celebrate their success and their acceptance of and by society.

Trimalchio's tomb would not have been to everyone's taste and Petronius makes it deliberately tacky. Indeed, by the later first century CE, extravagance at death may have been frowned on by the élite who, despite their often false humanity, would be anxious not to demean themselves by acting like ex-slaves! Remember the comments of both Pliny and Seneca about the heights of luxury and its negative and inappropriate elements.

These opinions may also have pervaded the funerary sphere. Certainly Stoic philosophy upheld the view that excessive mourning was unnecessary and self-indulgent and that death should be faced with equanimity (see Essay Seven, 'Seneca: a philosophy of living'). Seneca viewed funerary monuments as futile, seeing only literary works as being able to stand the ravages of time:

> And too, prolong the remembrance of your brother by some memorial in your writings; for among human achievements this is the only work that no storm can harm, nor length of time destroy. All others, those that are formed by piling up stones and masses of marble, or rearing on high huge mounds of earth, do not secure a long remembrance, for they themselves will also perish; but the fame of genius is immortal.
>
> (Seneca, *To Polybius on Consolation* 18.2, in Basore, 1932, p.411)

After his suicide Seneca was cremated without ceremony as he had directed in his will (Tacitus, *Annals* 15.62, in Grant. 1956).

Pliny's letters also contain some interesting musings on the role of monuments and how memory should best be preserved. For example, note *Letter* 3.21 in which Pliny sees the potential of Martial's poem for conveying immortality (as discussed in CD5).

Exercise

Read Pliny, *Letters* 6.10 and 9.19.

1   How does Pliny regard funerary monuments?

2   What was the opinion of Frontinus?

Verginius Rufus (CE 14–97) earned fame in CE 68 when, as governor of Germania Superior, he defeated a revolt led by Vindex, but did not attempt to unseat the emperor Nero.

Frontinus was a general and consul in CE 73, 98 and 100. He was also an author and published a work on Rome's aqueducts.

Discussion

1   Pliny is generally well disposed to the idea of the funerary monument and its associated epitaph. He writes of the tomb of his friend Verginius Rufus and is shocked that some time after his death it has still not been completed. He describes the tomb as modest, even humble and adds no details on its form apart from the epitaph. These words are of particular importance to Pliny since Verginius had penned them himself. In Pliny's opinion,

Figure 4.5 Front of the funerary altar of the freed slave Gaius Munatius Faustus from the Herculaneum Gate cemetery, Pompeii, first century BCE. Photo: Deutsches Archäologisches Institut, Rome/Nachlass Hofmann, Inst. Neg. no. 31.2780. Beneath the epitaph the deceased is depicted distributing corn or money to a crowd of people.

Figure 4.6 East side panel of the funerary altar of the freed slave Gaius Munatius Faustus from the Herculaneum Gate cemetery, Pompeii, first century BCE. Photo: Deutsches Archäologisches Institut, Rome/Rossa, Inst. Neg. no. 77.2129. This side exhibits a double seat awarded as a privilege to the deceased.

Figure 4.7   West side panel of the funerary altar of the freed slave Gaius Munatius Faustus from the Herculaneum Gate cemetery, Pompeii, first century BCE. Photo: Deutsches Archäologisches Institut, Rome/Rossa, Inst. Neg. no. 77.2184. This side shows a boat which may refer to some aspect of the deceased's occupation or represent the journey to the afterlife.

Verginius should have built the actual tomb himself because heirs are often unreliable. In the second letter Pliny defends Verginius' desire for a suitable tomb and epitaph. He believes Verginius deserved his memorial, especially such a modest one.

2   Allegedly Frontinus said 'A monument is money wasted; my memory will live on if my life has deserved it.' Pliny does not view this as a particularly reticent or modest thing to have said! But it illustrates that a funerary monument – especially some sort of extravagant building – was not always considered essential to the construction of the posthumous identity of the educated élite.

Funerary monuments and epitaphs are a fascinating source because of the insights they provide about very different people. Here we have the names and faces of people beyond the élite, who were eager to leave some lasting impression of themselves and/or their loved ones. But as with all evidence, we cannot isolate it from its wider context. When we read Pliny's letters, we ask questions about date, genre, intended audience and the social milieu of the author. We must apply the same methodology to an epitaph or funerary monument. Context is the key element. The funerary monument could present an individual's view of the world and construct a particular identity and impression of those named, presenting them in a certain fashion, prioritising pieces of information (names, ages, titles) over others. Choosing what to say or what to represent was a selective process. Funerary monuments were also the products of specific times and fashions. The mausoleum of Augustus was characteristic of its time, as was Frontinus' reluctance to have any tomb.

1.6 Conclusion

A recurrent theme of this first part of the block has been the importance of detecting the élite bias so dominant in our written sources. Epitaphs and tombstones do provide some differing perspectives, but as a source they are constrained by convention and societal expectations. Epitaphs and funerary monuments also formed part of the élite debate and dialogue that has featured strongly here. For Pliny there were certain ways of behaving – an élite code of conduct if you like – which influenced who he dined with, how he treated his slaves and even the type of funerary monument that he would receive. What Pliny said was not always followed or endorsed by others, but in his letters we see elements of an élite consensus on what defined and differentiated the élite from others in Roman society. For the social historian the challenge is how to access these 'others'. Knowing what Pliny said and did – or at least his representation and interpretation of his thoughts and actions – is not enough. We need to question the evidence of his letters and challenge the impressions they give by using additional sources and acknowledging that others, often suppressed and silenced, had differing perspectives and experiences.

Part 2 The Roman family

In this part of Block 4 we will explore issues and evidence relating to the Roman family. How can the Roman family both be investigated and understood? Your work is divided into three sections. In Section 2.1 you will consider how the Roman family can be defined and explore some of the ideals associated with Roman marriage. In Section 2.2 you will focus on one member of the family – the child – and evaluate our understanding of Roman childhood. In Section 2.3 you will consider familial representations at death in condolence letters and funerary memorials.

You will continue to work with primary sources, some of which – such as letters, epitaphs and funerary monuments – will be familiar from Part 1, while others – such as portraiture and consolation literature – will be new. There will be a continued emphasis on looking at evidence in context. In Part 1, the élite and educated bias to the literary sources was made apparent. Similar biases influence how we study the Roman family, but in this case we become particularly conscious of biases created by gender. In this part of the block you will also work with some short extracts from secondary sources, which will enable you to experience some aspects of academic debate and the differing conclusions drawn by modern scholars when using primary sources.

2.1 Defining the Roman family

This section explores what 'family' meant to a 'Roman' and how the Roman family has and can be studied. This raises some complex issues because the meaning of 'family' is not always easy to define. If you think of your own family you can begin to see the fluidity in both the definition and reality of family connections. How do you distinguish between those relations who are resident with you and those who are not? How has your resident family changed over the years? Perhaps you recently lived with your parents, or maybe your children have now left home. How often do you see or visit distant or even close relations? In many cultures and languages the meaning of 'family' is dependent on context.

I would now like you to read a passage from Cicero taken from a work called *On Duties* which Cicero wrote ostensibly for his son's benefit in 46 BCE.

Exercise

Read Cicero, *On Duties* 1.53–54 in Reading 4.9.

As you read, note the types of family relationships that Cicero lists. Are there any relationships missing?

Discussion

Cicero states that human society is divided by several means. One of the most fundamental of these is the bond between relations. First comes marriage and the relationship between husband and wife; then the relationship between parents and children; then the household unit (*domus*), 'the seed-bed of the state'; then relationships between siblings and cousins; then there are also relationships through marriage, non-blood connections. These ties 'force men to help and care for one another'. Cicero does not explicitly mention the ties between grandparents and grandchildren, or the relationship between aunts and uncles on the one hand, and nephews and nieces on the other.

Cicero makes it clear that relationships are important, especially to a male citizen with responsibilities to perpetuate the family name, promote the state and create personal and political alliances. Cicero defines differing levels of closeness and habitation. He identifies a central core of husband, wife and children (and slaves – see later). However, you may have noticed that this passage from Cicero does not contain the word 'family'. Indeed, confusion can arise when discussing the Roman family since there is no direct equivalent of the English word 'family' in ancient Latin. In the Roman world, was there a sense of family at all? Is what Cicero is describing a concept of family that we can understand and relate to? Indeed, you may even wish to challenge whether we should be asking questions such as this in the first place. In other words, are we so confined and conditioned by our own experiences and expectations of family life that we cannot look at the Roman world objectively?

Exercise

To introduce the problems of definition and some key Latin terms I would like you to read a short extract written by a modern scholar. This is taken from the first few pages of a book entitled *The Roman Family* by Suzanne Dixon.

Read the extract in Reading 4.24. As you read:

1   identify the key Latin terms;

2   evaluate how modern scholars have defined the Roman family.

Discussion

1　Here is a list of key terms derived from the passage:

> *familia* – this is not simply an equivalent of the English word 'family'. It was often used in legal contexts and usually referred to slaves and freed slaves;
>
> *paterfamilias* – father of the 'family', who had power over its members including children (*filiifamilias*, *filiaefamilias*) and slaves;
>
> *materfamilias* – mother of the 'family' – the wife of the *paterfamilias* was only referred to as this if she entered into her husband's *manus* (literally, hand) or power. If she did not, her legal ties remained with her natal family;
>
> *domus* – house and home, but also household. This is the term most often employed in Latin when referring to the lineage or kinship unit.

2　Dixon explains that defining and understanding the Roman family has been a subject of debate among social historians of the ancient world. If legal evidence is focused on, especially, 'the wide-ranging powers of the Roman *paterfamilias*', then the Roman family might be viewed 'as a three-generation household', with a patriarchal male exercising supreme power over his wife and children (including married sons and any grandsons). However, looking beyond legal sources to literary evidence suggests that such households were 'atypical'. By the mid-1980s, 'the prevailing view was that the Roman family was nuclear'.

There were two main reasons why I asked you to read the extract from Dixon's book:

1　Dixon provides a relatively user-friendly introduction to some important Latin terms. You could have been asked to read the *OCCC* entry on 'family, Roman' instead, and at some stage you may find it helpful to look at this. The *OCCC* entry is useful, but it is densely written and introduces many Latin terms. At this stage it is sufficient to focus on the handful of key terms identified by Dixon. However, there is an important issue at stake here: this is, that defining the Roman family can be complex. Much of this complexity lies in the law (remember the Augustan legislation on marriage and adultery examined in Block 3, Part 5). When we think of family we tend to focus on emotional bonds, but family is also underpinned and to some extent determined by law. One of the challenges in investigating family in the Roman world is to understand the balance between emotional bonds, legal niceties and other factors, such as economic necessities.

2 Dixon also introduces the idea of scholarly debate and this too has a legal dimension. As social history, as a discipline, has become more widely studied, the types of questions being asked have changed. There has been a move away from strict legal definitions of family, and different types of evidence have been investigated from a social perspective. You do not need to know all the debates for your work on this course, but you do need to be aware of how primary sources are used and how people can draw different conclusions from them.

To understand how the Roman 'family' functioned, scholars have sought to make the unfamiliar familiar by employing contemporary terminology. The term 'nuclear family' is a modern one and was certainly not employed in the Roman context, no more than was its opposite, the 'extended family'. Modern terms can be useful in allowing us to 'imagine' the Roman family, its constituent members, how they lived together and how they may have interacted. But we should be wary of equating the Roman family to the modern western ideal of the nuclear family with its affectionate ties and nominal equality between conjugal partners. Remember that many Roman households contained slaves – the *familia*, as outlined in Dixon's passage – which extended the 'family'. These slaves might form bonds with each other, creating 'families' – not legally recognised as such to be sure – within the *familia* (Figure 4.8). You were also probably struck by the supreme power (in Latin *potestas*) of the *paterfamilias*. The reality was – and this is suggested by the literary rather than legal sources – that the *paterfamilias* rarely employed the full range of his powers, such as the right to execute his sons. In fact, many fathers would not have lived long enough to see their sons reach adulthood, certainly not their grandsons, and so paternal interference in their lives may have been minimal. Yet economic resources were still concentrated in the hands of the *paterfamilias* and thus the Roman family was not a place of equality.

Something else you might like to consider when employing modern labels to describe the Roman family is the appropriateness of these across time and social status. For those citizen families without wealth the father's overarching powers may have counted for little, and the powerlessness of slave families has already been noted. In terms of time, consider how this affected every family. Children grew up, parents aged and died, slaves were freed – a family was constantly evolving and changing. Nor was the constitution and concept of the family necessarily static across time – *manus* marriage, for example, is thought to have declined in popularity by the late republic (see below). So people would have had varying experiences of

Figure 4.8   Funerary portrait relief of three freed slaves (Sextus Maelius Stabilio, Vesinia Iucunda and Sextus Maelius Faustus), early first century CE, 69.9cm x 170.2cm x 38.1cm. North Carolina Museum of Art, Raleigh. Purchased with funds from the State of North Carolina. A man and a woman grasp right hands (*dextrarum iunctio*), a traditional symbol of faithfulness and companionship in marriage. A second man – their son – is pictured adjacent to the woman. The epitaph reads: 'Sextus Maelius Stabilio, freedman of Sextus; Vesinia Iucunda, the freedwoman of a woman; Sextus Maelius Faustus, freedman of Sextus'.

family life depending on their social status, gender, age and period in which they lived.

The term 'nuclear family' is not wholly appropriate in the Roman context, but its use does allow us to explore a normative experience: to evaluate who lived with whom and for how long and thus how the generations may have interacted. Indeed, recent scholarship has moved away from assessing overall family form and has focused more on individuals such as children, mothers and the elderly, and on their experiences of family life. What we can say is that however it was defined or thought of, 'family' (or perhaps more accurately 'family relationships') did matter to the Romans. Dixon states that they 'saw family as central to their personal lives and to society'. The passage from Cicero's *On Duties*, read at the start of this section, makes it clear that familial relationships were the basis of the community and its bonds.

In the next section you will explore one group within the family – children – and their relationship with their parents and other carers. To end this section I wish briefly to consider the central relationship between husband and wife and the ideals associated with marriage. This will serve to introduce some of the challenges of accessing Roman family life through the available sources.

Cicero identifies marriage as fundamental to society's desire to propagate (Reading 4.9). Marriage was a way of ensuring legitimate heirs and thus sustaining the citizen body. If two Roman citizens each had the consent of the *paterfamilias* and lived together with the intention of being married, this was recognised as a valid marriage and children born of the union would be Roman citizens. Marriages united people, creating social, political and economic bonds between families. Property was of central importance, at least to those who had it. The wife provided a dowry which had to be repaid if the marriage ended. If the wife married *cum manu* (literally 'with hand/power'), she entered into the power of her husband's family. She could not possess property in her own right and she lost the right to intestate succession in her natal family. Marrying *sine manu* (literally, 'without hand/power') kept the woman under the authority of her father and she could inherit along with her siblings. By the late republic *sine manu* marriage had become the norm. Why the shift away from *cum manu* marriage occurred is unclear, but it may have been connected to the higher profile of upper-class women and the increased frequency of divorce.

Marriages among the wealthy élite – about whom we know the most – were arranged. The bride could not be forced to marry against her will, but may often have wished to please her parents, especially on a first marriage. There could also be a great inequality between the ages of spouses as women were married at a younger age than men. Many marriages would have ended with the death of one of the partners and many widowers and widows remarried. Divorce was also fairly frequent, at least among the élite, and was a relatively uncomplicated procedure. Serial marriage was common and many unions may have sprung from economic or political realities. Roman marriage was, then, a familial decision and not one based on the preferences of individuals influenced by personal attraction.

Inevitably such a brief summary of Roman marriage simplifies and compresses information and sources. If you wish to know more I suggest you begin with the *OCCC* entry on 'marriage law'. For the purposes of your study here I have simply emphasised the key features of Roman marriage to enable you to work with some primary evidence.

Exercise

Read:

- Cicero, *Letter to his family* (18) and *Letter to Atticus* 41, in Reading 4.1.[3]

- Pliny, *Letters* 4.19 and 7.5.

How useful are these letters as a source for evaluating and understanding the relationships between husbands and wives?

Discussion

Cicero and Pliny need little introduction at this stage of the course, but do remember their relative dates. Here we see some chronological continuity in the idealisation of husband and wife relations. Note how Pliny characterises Calpurnia as a good wife. She is caring, devoted, admiring, a good housewife and possibly a little subservient. This can be contrasted with Cicero's description of his sister-in-law's behaviour. Cicero and Pliny also both speak touchingly of the pain of separation and evoke a sense of love for their absent wives. Despite being arranged marriages, there appears to have been an expectation of genuine affection and even the prospect of romantic love.

The difficulty of using these letters to illustrate Roman marriage centres on issues of genre. As always we need to be aware that people and events are being presented in a certain way. Pliny, in particular, creates a literary portrait of an ideal wife and marriage. His wife and how she behaves, especially towards himself, is part of Pliny's own public image construction. Pliny was hardly going to use the medium of letter writing, especially a published letter to his wife's aunt, to complain about his wife's shortcomings and any marital disharmony! Cicero's letters reveal more about his private world and that of his brother, especially in his description of the discord between Pomponia and Quintus. We may question whether this particular letter was intended for publication! Cicero's observations are coloured by his desire to put his brother in a good light, thus we don't get to hear Pomponia's side of the argument. But at least the letter suggests that wives were not always passive. Indeed, in Cicero's absence his wife

[3] Terentia was Cicero's wife and Tullia and Marcus his children. Atticus was Cicero's closest friend, and Atticus's sister (Pomponia) was married to Cicero's brother, Quintus. See note 1 for numbering of Cicero's letters.

Terentia is supposed to fight his corner rather than weep for him hopelessly.

The letters are suggestive of various elements of Roman marriage – love, affection, devotion, dependency, anger and disappointment. They suggest ideals (and counter ideals) and paint a picture of how relationships should be rather than how they may actually have been. The ideals presented here only reflect the world of élite and educated men.

Pliny and Cicero may have loved their wives, but the letters they write reveal only some idealised aspects of their relationship. Our reading of these letters also becomes coloured by other things we can establish about these men and their family lives. Cicero and Terentia would eventually divorce and their subsequent relationship would not be on good terms. Cicero remarried a much younger wife, but this relationship ended in divorce within a few months. Quintus and Pomponia would also divorce. Calpurnia was the third wife of Pliny the Younger, previously widowed twice. Look at letter 4.19 again. You may notice that Pliny characterises his wife in rather a childlike fashion; indeed, Calpurnia was a teenager at the time of her marriage to Pliny, who was in his forties.

In this section we have noted the difficulties of defining the Roman family in simple terms. To understand family dynamics and interactions, modern scholars have described the Roman family as nuclear. Indeed, Cicero identifies the relationship between husband, wife and children as central to Roman society. As your work on Part 2 progresses, you should continue to evaluate how useful modern labels are as a means to access Roman family relationships. In looking at primary sources, and quizzing them for details on aspects of family life such as marriage, we are constantly made aware of issues of context. One of the most striking elements when addressing family matters is the gender bias. We may know how a man perceived his wife, or how he wished others to perceive her, but we rarely have the woman's perspective.

2.2 The Roman child

This section of the block will look at one particular member of the Roman family – the child – and at the historical accounts, ancient and modern, that contribute to our understanding of Roman childhood. To work on it you will need to refer to Essay Eight, 'The Roman Child', in *Experiencing the Classical World* and Readings Book 2. The aim of this section is to increase your understanding of the child's place in Roman society, of the importance of context in evaluating ancient primary sources, and of how modern historians may differ in the conclusions they draw or the emphases they make in using them. This section will concentrate on visual sources.

To begin, read through the following extract:

> Nevertheless, there are features which distinguish Roman society from any before it and from many later ones. [They] ... include the importance attached to education and sensitivity to the diversity of child development; the centrality of the conjugal family (spouses, sons and daughters) in expressions of sentiment and in many practical areas, e.g. law and housing; a wider network of surrogate family in which carers, slaves, and ex-slaves had an important place; a public life which stressed historical tradition and *exempla* (models) to guide a child's development and aspirations, and which provided entertainment and ritual which stimulated and socialized a child's responses; an unprecedentedly large and elaborate capital city full of visual and aural messages; a body of legislation and legal commentary in which children had an important place; and widespread, individualized funerary commemoration of children which emphasized the 'father–mother–children triad'.
>
> (Rawson, 2003, p.2)

Here Beryl Rawson, a historian of Roman childhood, records aspects of Roman society which, in her view, made Roman childhood distinctive. The passage provides you with a checklist of points to use as you make your own notes on Essay Eight in *Experiencing the Classical World*.

Please read Essay Eight in *Experiencing the Classical World*.

1   How far does Valerie Hope, its author, cover the points made by Rawson in her discussion of 'the Roman child'?

2   Are there other points that Hope stresses?

3   Are there questions that perhaps she downplays?

1   Essay Eight includes some discussion of almost all the distinctive points noted by Rawson, particularly those that deal with

surrogate childcare, with the differentiation of childhood as a separate (biological or legal) stage in life, and with the representation of children in a family context. It has less on the effects of public life on the socialization of children, although the quotation from Horace (*Satire* 1.6. 77–82) gives some interesting insights into the social accomplishments available at Rome, while the story of Aeneas provides a famous role model for the social virtue of *pietas*. The essay touches on education in several passages but without a separate discussion. (You can find a basic outline of Roman education in *OCCC*, pp.249–51.)

2   Turning to the second question, I would highlight three features that Hope stresses in Essay Eight:

(a)   children in relation to different social levels in Roman society: in particular, 'an emperor's childhood' and children in freedmen families;

(b)   the Roman relationship of *potestas*, and in particular the lifelong legal powers this gave the father (*patria potestas*);

(c)   exposure and abandonment: a social practice distinctive to ancient society.

Together these three points make important contributions to the discussion of the topic. The first is a reminder of how much the experience of childhood must have varied according to social status, as well as across time and place, in the Roman world (see Essay Eight, 'The Roman child', pp.173–74). The other two points are distinctive aspects of Roman attitudes towards childhood which may seem negative to us and which have found a place in a certain modern argument about the history of Roman childhood (influenced by the work of Philippe Ariès; see Essay Eight, p.176). But it is vital that we try to understand these attitudes towards children in their proper historical context. Hope makes important points about this in her section on 'The impact of early death' (Essay Eight, pp.187–89) and I will return to this later.

3   It could be argued that the essay downplays two important aspects of Roman childhood: namely, age and gender. Both were important factors, then as since, in how children were perceived and treated. But although the essay has no separate sections on these issues, it does make a number of important points about them which you might usefully note as you read.

From looking at the coverage of topics to do with childhood, we turn now to the ancient sources of evidence from which our knowledge is derived. Rawson mentions, for instance, legislation, funerary commemoration and the practicalities of housing, which are all likely sources of solid information about childhood. However, I find it hard to know how we might ascertain Roman children's responses to their 'unprecedently large and elaborate capital city full of visual and aural messages'. This is a particular case in which we have to lament the fact that 'Roman children in general have not left us their voices' (Essay Eight, p.174): a child's reaction to the Colosseum and the games would have been fascinating!

The fact that none of our evidence preserves the voices of Roman children themselves has far-reaching implications for our study, as Hope examines in the section of the essay entitled 'The voice of the child' (pp.174–77). All the evidence now available to us was interpreted or generated by adults and we need to assess their motives and viewpoints carefully, 'with a constant awareness of their original context, purpose and audience' (Essay Eight, p.175). The two short exercises that follow emphasise this, and involve comparing some visual images of children and rereading parts of Essay Eight.

Exercise

Reread Essay Eight, 'The voice of the child' (pp.174–77). As you read, note examples of where the ancient evidence might have been biased by gender, idealisation, social or economic standing. Also note the purpose of the source.

Discussion

These are all factors that have been discussed earlier in this block, and which are especially important in considering visual representations of the child. So often these were made by and for the wealthy, urban, freeborn élite, and by men who would have had limited involvement in children's everyday lives.

Exercise

Now compare four different images: Figure 8.1 from Essay Eight (p.175), and Figures 4.9, 4.10 and 4.11 below. How are the children represented (e.g. in terms of dress, gesture etc.) What can be said about them in terms of gender, age and social status?

Figure 4.9   Statue of Nero as a boy from Velleia group of the imperial family, *c.*CE 50, Museo Nazionale di Antichità, Parma, inv. no. 826. Photo: Deutsches Archäologisches Institut, Rome, Inst. Neg. no. 67.1587.

Figure 4.10   Funerary monument of the boy poet Quintus Sulpicius Maximus, *c.*CE
94, Palazzo Nuovo, Capitoline Museums, Rome, inv. no. 1102. Photo: Deutsches
Archäologisches Institut, Rome/Singer, Inst. Neg. no. 71.1964. The inscription on the
base reads: 'Sacred to the departed spirit of Q. Sulpicius Maximus, son of Quintus and
of the Claudian tribe, a native of Rome. He lived for eleven years, five months and
twelve days. He took part at the third celebration of the competition, amongst 52
Greek poets and the favour which he attracted through his tender age was turned to
admiration by his talent. He departed with honour. His extemporaneous verses are set
out above so that his parents should not look as if they are indulging their affections.
Q. Sulpicius Eugramus and Licinia Ianuaria his most unhappy and devoted parents set
up the monument to him, to themselves and to their successors.'

Figure 4.11   Funerary monument of Nico and Eutyches, early second century CE, Villa Albani, Rome. Photo: Deutsches Archäologisches Institut, Rome. Inst Neg. no. EA4533. The inscription records that it was dedicated by Publicia Glypte to the departed spirits of Nico, her sweetest son, who lived for eleven months and eight days, and Eutyches, a slave born in the household, who lived one year, five months and ten days.

Discussion

Two of these monuments were funerary memorials to children who had died; the other two are statues of a young boy who was to become emperor. Figure 4.9 of Nero as a child is very similar to Figure 8.1 in Essay Eight. We do not know where the statue shown in Figure 8.1 was discovered, but that shown in Figure 4.9 is especially significant as it is part of a group of statues commemorating the imperial family found in the northern Italian town of Velleia. The group was probably dedicated by the city of Velleia and was on public display during the first century CE. It was updated from time to time by adding new members of the dynasty, or even by recarving the heads of some statues to create new portraits. The statue of Nero in Figure 4.9 seems to have been added just after his adoption by the emperor Claudius in CE 50 (and just before the year in which he would have given up wearing the *bulla* on taking up the *toga virilis* – see Essay Eight, p.177). The statue was assembled rather than a specially carved: a portrait head of Nero was simply added to a secondhand body of a boy wearing a *bulla*. But even so it had a particularly urgent political purpose – to bring the young Nero into public view as an important future player in the imperial dynasty.

What is immediately striking about all four images is their great similarity in terms of pose, dress, gestures and attributes. There may be small differences (such as Nero's *bulla*), but otherwise the figures are shown dressed in togas and standing, holding out scrolls (this is probably how the Velleia Nero in Figure 4.9 stood before the forearms were damaged). Quintus Sulpicius Maximus (Figure 4.10) has his scroll half-opened as if he was declaiming from his prize-winning poetry (which is inscribed on the monument around his figure), while the other images include a cylindrical scroll-box at the figures' feet.

This particular type of statue was very common in Roman art to represent the male citizen: the statues at Velleia, for instance, represented male members of the imperial family in this way, but with togas drawn up over their heads to represent religious piety (see, for example, Germanicus in Figure 4.12). But although the figures of these children follow this adult model, the faces are mainly childish and rounded in shape and, as one might expect from imperial portraits, there is a recognisable similarity between the two portraits of the young Nero, with a heart-shaped face and a fringe falling from a central parting, and wearing the *bulla*.

With this visual similarity in mind, what can be said about the individuals represented in terms of their gender, age and social status?

Figure 4.12   Statue of Germanicus from Velleia group of the imperial family, *c*.CE 50, Museo Nazionale de Antichità, Parma, inv. no. 832. Photo: Deutsches Archäologisches Institut, Rome/Singer, Inst. Neg. no 67.1596.

To state the obvious, they are all boys: girls were commemorated on funerary memorials, but often with different imagery relevant to their roles in Roman society. We can see that the boys range in age from Nico aged eleven months to Nero who was probably about thirteen years old at the time. Yet this same adult-figure type is used for them all, irrespective of age or even of physical reality. The image of the two young infants is a clear pointer to this: despite the scrolls they are depicted with, they would have been illiterate, and were probably unable to stand erect and unaided like this, whether dressed in togas or not. As Rawson says: 'The representation of Eutyches is especially optimistic, as a slave would not normally look forward to a liberal education or a toga' (2003, p.261). So in this case we might conclude that the images were not meant to be realistic but somehow symbolic – an impression enhanced by the image in the pediment of a hind suckling a small child in Figure 4.11). This may have been intended to evoke how the little slave was fostered by Publicia Glypte almost as a brother to her son Nico. Certainly there is a good deal of scope to interpret the scenes on this monument in a symbolic way. But the memorial to Quintus Sulpicius Maximus may be different: the eleven-year old poet may well have already cultivated the adult stance of a performer at public competitions, making his image perhaps a little closer to reality although its overall appearance is undeniably adult. As for the portraits of Nero, some supposedly individual features would have been required to emphasise his dynastic role in the imperial family, even if in fact he did not look exactly as portrayed. So taken together, these images are more symbolic than naturalistic. In terms of social status they cover a wide range, from Eutyches, who was a *verna* (a slave born within a household), to Nero, the potential heir to the empire, showing that their common figure-type is no real indicator of social status.

So why was it quite so popular for boys across a range of ages and social positions to be commemorated in this way? The answer must be that it was important to project this model image of the adult citizen male. The figure-type in these monuments served to represent adult hopes and expectations projected on to boys who had died prematurely (expressed most acutely perhaps in the memorial to Quintus Sulpicius Maximus) and also suggested social qualities of Roman manhood that lay ahead for the child. These boys and their families were depicted in adult society, whether as future rulers, as members of an educated and literate élite, or with a place within the Roman household.

To sum up, this exercise has shown how children – in this case, boys – may often be represented by rather stereotypical figures based on adult models. This can result in visual images that may look very similar and also express some common attitudes to childhood (in representing it in terms of adult social values but sometimes with different features such as a childlike physique or a special sign of status). Yet to understand the individual value of each representation it is vital to look outside the visual image to other contextualising evidence: for instance, it is only from their accompanying inscriptions that we learn the particular background to the life and death of Quintus Sulpicius Maximus, or the age and different social ranks of the two infants Nico and Eutyches. It is vital that we consider the context and purpose of the surviving sources of evidence for Roman childhood.

It would be wrong to take away from this exercise the impression that this 'adult' mode was the only way of depicting children, or that it was exclusive to boys. Girls too were shown with the attributes of mature women, like the hairstyle worn by the young girl shown reclining on a sarcophagus lid (Figure 4.13), and both boys and girls were represented looking much more like children in many portraits, especially of infants. The age of the small girl Ammaea Urbana (Figure 4.14) is not given in the epitaph inscribed by her parents, but her portrait suggests she may have been two or three years old.

The next exercise looks at some images of young boys shown in a family context.

Exercise

Reread the section of Essay Eight entitled 'Defining the child'.

How do the two monuments illustrated in Figures 8.2 and Figures 8.3 in Essay Eight 'define' the child? What are their similarities and differences? The features you should concentrate on are physical characteristics, activities and the relationship with parents.

Discussion

In terms of similarities, both are funerary memorials which commemorate young boys through a combination of visual image and text: the inscriptions give the children's names and social status, and the images show each child in a family context with his parents. Both monuments attempt to depict the children as physically different from the adults: note their smaller size and more rounded heads, which in the case of Globulus is accentuated to an almost grotesque degree. Status is obviously an important issue as both inscriptions make clear; and as with Nero in the first exercise, the *bulla* worn by Globulus is

Figure 4.13   Artist unknown, Kline monument with a Reclining Girl, c.CE 120–140, marble, 38cm x 47cm x 141cm, The J. Paul Getty Museum, Villa Collection, Malibu, California. © The J. Paul Getty Museum. The young girl is reclining on a sarcophagus lid.

Figure 4.14   Altar of Ammaea Urbana, Museo Nazionale, Rome. Photo: Deutsches Archäologisches Institut, Rome/Singer, Inst. Neg. no 72.3026.

significant as it distinguishes his free birth and also that he is still a child.

By emphasising these features these portraits form part of the body of evidence which suggests that Romans did, indeed, perceive childhood as a particular period of human life – distinct from adulthood, yet closely allied to it. Although Globulus is separated by a pillar from his parents, he is still part of the same family group and is portrayed with similar dress and gestures. The sarcophagus (Figure 8.3) provides even further evidence as the whole image is couched in terms of activities typical of childhood's separate stages: babyhood, play and education are acted out in suitable situations under the parents' ever-watchful eyes.

Yet despite these attempts at a 'realistic' representation of children's physical differences, the images also idealise certain aspects of childhood. This is particularly clear in the events depicted on the sarcophagus which apparently shows Statius in training for the adult life of the élite, to which he sadly failed to survive. Even his play in a chariot is reminiscent of serious adult activities, while the scene of him apparently declaiming in front of his father definitely looks ahead to successful participation in adult public life. (Did you notice how he is shown with a toga and scroll like the boys in the earlier exercise?) As part of this narrative his parents are also represented in idealised terms as they participate in his upbringing in a 'hands-on' way, which runs counter to the written historical accounts in which surrogate carers play a large role (as summarised in Essay Eight, the section entitled 'Caring for the child', pp.184–87). In Figure 8.3, Statius' mother breastfeeds him herself and his father is involved in his education. Parental pride and desire to illustrate the level of their concern for their son may perhaps have been the motive for this image; and these sentiments can also be sensed in the depiction of Globulus, in which the *bulla* shows that as freeborn, he was already higher up the social scale than his parents who were freed slaves.

Despite these similarities in the purpose and general ethos of the monuments, the images are strikingly different in style and content. Globulus and his parents stare out uncompromisingly at the viewer, set side by side in static and rather formulaic poses. In many ways Globulus looks like a little adult. In contrast, Statius is depicted at various stages of his short life including babyhood. He and his family are shown in naturalistic and informal poses, and the episodes of his life unfold in an organic, chronological sequence without any apparent reference to the onlooker. Yet, as we have already seen, appearances may be deceptive: a comparison with other examples in art and literature shows that these scenes are, in fact, artfully chosen and composed to reinforce the familiar message of an ideal home life based on simple 'family values'. They are neither a random selection of episodes, nor snapshots of this individual family's home life, but, in their own way, they are as conventional and formulaic as the image on the tomb-building relief.

One reason for the very different visual effects of the two images is to be found in the particular ways in which the monuments were used and positioned. The relief showing Globulus and his parents was probably placed on the outside of a tomb building to show who was buried within to passers-by; the sarcophagus, on the other hand, was designed to contain the child's body, and would have been placed inside a burial chamber. The relief, therefore, was intended for public display whereas the sarcophagus would have been seen by a much smaller circle of family visitors and friends. This might explain why the scene on the sarcophagus gives an intimate picture of the boy in a family setting, while the relief looks far more like a public statement about social status and identity. Here again it is important to note how the aims and contexts of the images were very different.

Finally, what can be said about these monuments in terms of the various biases we considered earlier? Idealisation and social standing have already been mentioned. Economic factors are important: monuments like these were only erected by the relatively wealthy, and the images of Statius' childhood suggest that he came from a family which could afford to give their son a leisured childhood and training for an élite career (and had the social aspirations to do so). As for gender, the fact that yet again the images depict boys is significant; although girls were also commemorated on comparable monuments, they appear far less frequently. Clearly families who could afford such monuments thought it important to commemorate their sons, and in terms that celebrated their social status and looked ahead – even implicitly – to new generations of the family. The context of funerary commemorations meant that these themes were couched in particular conventions. Another factor to consider is the date of each of these pieces. The grave relief (Figure 8.2) belongs to a series that was used particularly by newly freed slaves to commemorate their families: status was all important. The sarcophagus (Figure 8.3) was made about 150 years later, by which time it had become fashionable for family monuments of all kinds to celebrate personal affection and private family relationships (see Essay Eight, p.178, and DVD4,

Section 1, 'Roman funerary monuments'). Sentiment replaces civic standing as the prime thing to commemorate.

There are two wider issues you should consider in your work on Roman childhood. The first concerns the difficulties involved in dealing with scattered ancient evidence. The second is to do with different readings and interpretations that modern scholars may attribute to ancient material. Both are highly relevant to the study of many other topics in ancient social history, and the Roman family makes a useful case study.

Scattered evidence and unanswered questions are discussed at various points in Essay Eight. Working with evidence of this kind is difficult and it is important to be clear about not only what is represented and why, but also about the gaps and silences in the evidence. The lack of surviving evidence for a particular situation is no reason to conclude that the particular situation did not exist. Yet piecing together disparate pieces of surviving evidence requires care and skill – and also acceptance that some vital questions will have to remain unanswered. However, the lack of answers does not invalidate the questions themselves: it is important to go on asking them and to consider fresh interpretations of the material that does remain.

Here we move on to the second point. As scholars ask new questions of the same, patchily surviving material, different interpretations and views emerge which in turn may be questioned and redefined. The study of Roman childhood contains a particularly powerful example, as described in Essay Eight (pp.176–87). Deriving from Ariès' influential work on childhood, it has been suggested that Romans were indifferent to childhood as a separate stage in life and also to the care and survival of their own individual children. Look back at Essay Eight for a fuller discussion of this view and the evidence on which it was based; but note how Hope asserts that in many ways this is an anachronistic approach, in which modern values are projected back on to the ancient situation with all its legal, economic and demographic complexities. Here is an important point which we need to take to heart when we think about ancient societies: just how far can we use our own cultural and moral values to illuminate a very different situation from our own, particularly when the evidence for that ancient society is so patchy? Is objectivity even possible? The answer is that there can be no right or definite answer. All we can do is ask appropriate questions, evaluate the evidence as carefully as we can in the hope that understanding its context may help towards a solution, and be aware that historical interpretations are, in fact, just that – they are not full answers or complete narratives, but readings of ancient evidence made from particular modern perspectives.

These are the kinds of modern value judgements and cultural assumptions that Hope rightly warns against (e.g. Essay Eight, p.173). For a study of childhood there is a further, even more personal factor to be aware of as we try to interpret the past – the experiences of our own childhood. We all have memories which will inevitably colour our responses to Roman childhood and our assumptions about it. But though these need to be kept to one side when we try to evaluate the ancient historical evidence on its own terms, they may help us to appreciate some of the tensions and ambiguities entailed in studying childhood in any historical period. For in thinking about children in general, we often deal in polar opposites – 'little angels' or 'little devils', 'innocence' or 'experience' – and this may help us to understand more readily why Roman attitudes to children often seem so ambivalent. (See the example of how Romans like Fronto could enjoy the particular qualities of young children, yet constantly look ahead to children's potential contribution as adult members of society, in Essay Eight; and something of this is reflected in the figure of the girl in Figure 4.13, which is so mature in some respects, yet is shown with dolls and a pet dog.) Even if Roman ambivalence was not quite the same as our own, here perhaps we can legitimately bring some personal understanding to our reading of the rather disparate primary evidence that exists for Roman childhood. Added to careful contextualisation of the ancient images and texts, it can help to develop useful and illuminating interpretations of Roman social history.

2.3   Death and the family

Family life was easily disrupted and disjointed. Divorce, exile, military service and slavery could all separate husbands and wives, parents and children. But above all, death took its toll. It was often in the shadow of death that ideals were created, and it is often these ideals that survive for us to study. Note the tomb reliefs that you looked at in the previous section and how these represented the dead children. In this section we will consider how dead family members were talked of, described and characterised through the media of consolation letters, epitaphs and funerary monuments. What ideals were created and what value does this evidence have for the social historian?

Condolence letters, sent to the bereaved, were an expected part of Roman public life. To show respect for the deceased and their survivors it was standard to send a letter of condolence, especially if you could not pay your respects in person. From this convention arose a stylised genre, which both praised the deceased and exhorted the living to be strong.

In 45 BCE Cicero's grown-up daughter Tullia died.

Exercise

Read Servius Sulpicius Rufus' letter to Cicero (Cicero, *Letter* 102 and Cicero's reply (Cicero, *Letter* 103),[4] both in Reading 4.1.

How does Servius Sulpicius Rufus offer comfort? Does the tone of the letter surprise you? How does Cicero characterise his grief?

Discussion

Cicero's grief runs deep. At times he is 'overwhelmed'. Servius Sulpicius Rufus acknowledge this great sense of loss and claims to share it. Many tears have been shed and offering comfort is challenging to those closest to the bereaved. Nevertheless Servius Sulpicius Rufus takes it on himself to offer some sensible advice. The tone of his letter is stern and moralising. In the grand scheme of things, and especially in the current climate, Tullia's death is not that great a calamity. Everyone dies. You may have found that, in parts, the letter seems harsh and lacking in compassion. You may also have been surprised that both men use the correspondence as a vehicle to bewail the decline of the republic and the political upheavals of the time. In some respects Tullia is lucky to have escaped life and all its present disappointments! There is little here on Tullia as a person, her achievements, hopes and aspirations, beyond, that is, her marriage prospects. She is Cicero's daughter and defined as such rather than as a person in her own right. For Cicero, the loss of his daughter runs parallel to and almost becomes a metaphor for his political impotence. Both his public and private life is under threat. Even the household which was once his refuge from politics is now in turmoil. Cicero clearly misses Tullia immensely; in her he had 'a haven of refuge and repose, one in whose conversation and sweet ways I put aside all cares and sorrows'. This is a touching if somewhat egocentric view of his loss.

You may find it useful to look back at Essay Six, 'Roman reputations', where Paula James also discusses these letters (pp.136–39). Note in particular the comment 'they [the letters] provide more than one kind of evidence for a student of the Roman Empire' (p.139). These letters have the potential to reveal many things; here we are looking at them from the perspective of social history, for what they reveal about the expression of grief and the characterisation of family relationships. But in doing this we

[4] See note 1.

immediately see that we cannot isolate the letters from the context of Cicero's life and the political backdrop of the late republic.

In public, men of Cicero's standing were expected to acknowledge their losses and then put their grief aside. Mourning could not be allowed to interfere with politics and the running of the state. Cicero might weep in private, but not in public. Condolence letters, especially anything that might be published, reflected this public ideal. Like many aspects of Roman life, how to grieve – how to dine, how to treat your slaves, your wife or your children – was part of an élite male discourse on how one should behave. We may read a condolence letter expecting emotion, love and loss, and these things are present, but they are mixed with other sterner sentiments.

Philosophy played its part in creating ideals for how one should both face one's own death and that of others. Seneca wrote many condolence letters and whole essays known as 'Consolations' on how to face bereavement. These were moralising works that were full of Stoic exhortations not to mourn in excess since everyone must die. (Note Cicero wrote a 'Consolation' after Tullia's death, but it does not survive, see *Letters to Atticus* 251 in Reading 4.10.)

Exercise

Read Seneca, *Moral Letters* 99, 1–6 and 14–18 in Reading 4.6.

You will also find it helpful to look back at Essay Seven, 'Seneca: a philosophy of living' in *Experiencing the Classical World*, especially the section 'Seneca on facing up to death' (pp.165–68).

How would you evaluate this letter as a source for the nature of grief and mourning in ancient Rome? Think about its context (e.g. who it was written for and why) and how its context shapes its content.

Discussion

It is challenging for a modern reader not to react negatively to parts of Seneca's letter. The tone can be harsh and unforgiving. A man has lost his infant son and Seneca dismisses the child as a 'fragment of time' and someone better known to his 'nurse' (*nutrix*) than his father. Otherwise the child is not mentioned or discussed. The child's death may be the root cause of the letter, but he is given no name or central role in it. All this seems very alien to how we would react to a child's death, but we need to remember the ancient context of child mortality and idealised behaviour. Look back to Essay Eight for further discussion of this. Indeed, the letter needs to be viewed in the context in which it is presented – a philosophical example of how to support and advise the bereaved. Seneca makes it clear that he deliberately chose to take a harsh line: 'I did not believe that he should be handled gently'. Equally Seneca does not completely dismiss the natural instinct for a father to mourn his son. Grief is a natural emotion, 'Tears fall, no matter how we try to check them'. Seneca's criticism is of 'indulgence in grief', of false tears, and of exaggerated and elongated displays of mourning. For Seneca, philosophical principles mean that grief is useless and thankless. All men will die and we should be thankful for what we have had rather than mourn for what we have lost.

Seneca focuses on philosophical ideals and provides insights into these. Men who view grief as useless and get straight back to politics are admired. Seneca also explores the counter ideal – those who indulge in public displays of grief. As is so often the case, the value of the letter lies in the insights it provides into ideals and stereotypes. Here we have the Stoic version of how one should mourn, not the reality of how one actually did. In opposition to this we have a polarised view of people so gripped by grief that they weep uncontrollably, throw themselves off couches and do themselves personal injury. Seneca explores two extremes of behaviour – one is presented as characteristic of the élite male and the other as characteristic of women and 'the mob'. What all this suggests is that certain behaviour was expected from different groups and becomes stereotyped accordingly. Seneca acknowledges that both extremes of behaviour are open to criticism, and thus for many people the reality may have been somewhere in between – to show emotion but not to an immoderate degree. The letter, then, provides insights into how people were expected to react to a child's death, how men should mourn, how women were allowed to express their grief and the perceived differences between the élite and 'the people'. A guide on how best to grieve for a child might have taken a very different tone if written by a poverty-stricken mother.

 Pliny also wrote letters on the deaths of certain acquaintances. These were not condolence letters as such, since they were not written to the bereaved but to friends of Pliny to inform them of the deaths. Since they were not addressed to the bereaved, in these letters Pliny had the freedom to moralise about the life of the deceased, express his own grief, and comment on the conventions of both mourning and condolence. Note *Letter* 8.16 which Pliny wrote on the deaths of his slaves, which you read earlier. In such a letter the literate Pliny has an opportunity to express his humanity. Another of Pliny's 'condolence' letters, written on the death of Minicia Marcella, is mentioned in Essay Eight. This is *Letter* 5.16 and you may wish to read it in full. Pliny paints a poignant picture of a girl who was on the point of adulthood and marriage at the time of her death. It is notable that the girl is not named in the letter, but simply referred to as the daughter of Fundanus. We know her name from a surviving epitaph which also reveals that Pliny probably had her age wrong (see Figure 4.15, DVD4 and the epitaph in Reading 4.8). This suggests the poetic licence that Pliny took in his writing – painting the right picture and creating the fitting tone was more important than factual accuracy. The letter ends by noting that Fundanus had been badly affected by his grief. Fundanus is described as a philosopher, but one who was now struggling to follow his own advice. Pliny suggests that any condolence letters written to Fundanus should not be too reproving (compare this with Seneca's view). Pliny ends by noting that, with time, Fundanus' perspective will change – time heals.

In reality, it could be difficult to live up to the ideal of how to grieve well. Public expectation might be in conflict with private emotion. Men were expected to take their familial bereavements with a stiff upper lip; excessive mourning was viewed as 'womanly'. But once more we have no direct literary insights into how women did grieve. Women are advised how to behave by men (see Seneca, *To Marcia on consolation*, in Reading 4.7) and their grief is described by men and often characterised as unrestrained in comparison to the behaviour admired by these male authors. (Compare as well Pericles advice to female mourners in Block 2.) At the very least we can say that not everyone (men and women) conformed to Seneca's strict expectations; this is suggested by the very fact that Seneca felt the need to write in the way he did. In other genres, poetry in particular, emotions could be heightened and the intensity of grief explored. But are such outbursts any more representative of how people behaved than the polarisation of behaviour found in Seneca's letters?

Can epitaphs and funerary monuments provide us with some useful or alternative insights? Cicero planned to build a memorial shrine to Tullia. He wrote several letters on this topic to his friend Atticus (*Letters to Atticus* 275 – in Reading 4.10). Remembering the dead was a duty, but it was one that must often have sprung from genuine affection. Cicero regarded the shrine as a debt to be paid. This memorial, which in the end was never built, was to promote the memory of his daughter. A tomb or tombstone served this purpose for most people. Central to the identity created at death for many was their role within the family as father, mother, daughter or son. Thousands of the epitaphs that survive from the city of Rome contain statements of familial relationships. The commemorator – that is, the person setting up the memorial – stated their name and relationship to the deceased. For examples, look at the epitaphs in Reading 4.8. Affectionate epithets were frequently employed – 'to my dearest son', 'the best husband',

Figure 4.15 Funerary altar of Minicia Marcella, 130cm x 70cm x 55cm, late first century CE. Museo Nazionale, Rome, inv. 217. Photo: Deutsches Archäologisches Institut, Rome/Rossa, Inst. Neg. no. 76.1732.

and so forth. Scantia Sabina is described as 'filiae pientissimae', a very pious or devoted daughter. Publicia Glypte set up a memorial to her 'sweetest son' (Figure 4.11).

Such simple expressions can be touching and moving. The modern reader may more readily relate to these epitaphs, and the sentiments they contain, than to the ideas and ideals of Seneca. Here we have real people giving expression to real losses, such as the mother's voice which was excluded from formal literature. However, epitaphs, like condolence letters, were influenced by public expectations and could idealise the dead and their relationships with the living. Was Publicia Glypte expressing her true feelings or just saying and doing what was expected? Did she compose the words of the epitaph and choose the image or did the stonemason guide or even control her decisions? We may not be able to answer these questions, but we can note that although conventional language may seem to trivialise the depth and individuality of grief, it does not mean that the grief was not heartfelt. Conventions and societal expectations, whether in the realm of philosophy or epitaphs, may structure and guide the expression of emotion, but they do not necessarily suppress it.

Latin epitaphs presented an ideal of family and family relationships, and part of this ideal was that the family should be buried and remembered together. The tomb of the Scipio family stretched across several generations (see Block 3). The powerful élite were supposed to preserve *imagines* (masks of their ancestors) and have portraits of successful forebears on display. Reality may have been somewhat different.

Exercise

You should now watch DVD4, Section 1, 'Roman funerary monuments' again and focus on the final two tracks. Refer to Audio-Visual Notes 2. At the same time, look at Plate 45 in the Illustrations Book (a plan of the tombs at Isola Sacra).

As you watch, reflect on the ways in which the living, especially the family, were supposed to interact with the dead.

Discussion

The tombs of the Isola Sacra provide some fascinating insights into how people were commemorated and remembered. Statements of family relationships were an important aspect of the epitaphs. Most of the relationships recorded were from the immediate family of husbands, wives, parents and children. But the epitaphs could look to the future by using imprecise formulae that gave burial rites to unnamed children and unnamed freed slaves. The tombs looked to the future – providing burial spaces for many people and specifying who (in generalised terms) could have access to these. The founders hoped the tomb would stay in the family, or more widely the *familia*, since ex-slaves also bore the family name. The more people who had a vested interest in the tomb, the more likely it was to be maintained and thus its 'inhabitants' remembered. The tombs were also designed to encourage the living to visit the dead and bring offerings. Wells, benches, dining areas and spaces for barbecues were sometimes integral to the design of the tomb. Some tombs were used for extended periods, but the wishes of the tomb founders may not have been followed exactly. The tombs evolved to meet changing needs –

they could be extended or divided, and burials spaces within them sold or given away.

Families died out and memory was, and is, a fickle thing. Few people living in ancient Rome could afford a grand family tomb. Even those who built them may not have used them for long. The surviving epitaphs focus on what was the here and now – husbands, wives, parents and children are named, but rarely is reference made to grandparents, grandchildren, aunts and uncles. Indeed, epigraphic evidence has been a mainstay in the debate about Roman family structure, employed as evidence to support the idea that the Roman family was 'nuclear' (see above). But this does not mean that the ideal of family continuity and respect for the ancestors was neglected and forgotten. People set up epitaphs and tombstones because they wanted to remember their dead and be remembered themselves; they hoped that people would continue to speak their name by reading their epitaph and that family – including slaves and freed slaves – would maintain and visit the grave.

The potential mismatch between ideal and reality is at its most poignant in the realm of death and mourning. Condolence letters, epitaphs and tombs all create ideals about how to grieve, how to remember the dead and the importance of family to the whole process. Death, grief, mourning and loss are presented in a certain, accepted and conventionalised fashion. What we have is not real Roman tears and emotions, but representations of these, which are important and revealing in their own right and have the potential to tell us a good deal about Roman society, its interactions and expectations.

2.4   Conclusion

In Part 2 we have focused on the Roman family. This has often been an emotive and challenging task. Even defining the Roman family is difficult and accessing all its constituent members is not straightforward. What we can access is an ideal of family life: the perfect wife, the perfect child, the perfect family mourner; and sometimes counter ideals, or at least what lay in opposition to the ideals upheld by the male élite.

When studying the ancient evidence relevant to family it can be difficult for us to shut down our own emotional responses to what we see and read. This may be heightened by ambivalent feelings toward modern ideals surrounding family and/or mourning for the dead. As historians we need to be objective – but we all have families (in some shape or form), we have all been children, we will all experience bereavement – and is it possible, or even desirable, to isolate completely our experiences from those of others? At the very least our diverse individual experiences may help us to appreciate the tensions, ideals and ambiguities that so often characterise family life in any period. However, in the context of ancient Rome we need to avoid making modern value judgements in our search to illuminate a society that could be very different from our own and for which the evidence is so often incomplete.

We need always to be aware of the original context and purpose of the evidence that we have. We cannot access all aspects of Roman family life, marriage, childhood or bereavement because the surviving evidence simply does not allow this. Equally, you may wish to question whether it is ever possible to understand fully what are primarily the emotional bonds of others. Accessing anyone else's feelings or emotions is always problematic, let alone across a divide of two thousand years. Some things, both as individuals and as historians, lie beyond our grasp. However, what we can investigate and seek to understand is how relationships and their emotional and practical (i.e. legal, economic etc.) dimensions are represented and characterised in the ancient evidence, and thus increase our overall understanding of Roman society.

Part 3 Living in Rome

In Part 3 you will explore issues and evidence relating to life in the city of Rome. Where did people live? How were public spaces and places used? Can we reconstruct how people interacted in private and in public? Your work is divided into three sections. In Section 3.1 you will consider evidence connected to housing in the city of Rome and the balance between public and private in the domestic sphere. In Section 3.2 you will evaluate the purpose of the circus, theatre and amphitheatre and how the audience reacted to and interacted at the events held there. In Section 3.3 you will consider the role of bathing and public baths in the social life of the city's inhabitants. You will continue to work with the sort of primary evidence introduced elsewhere in this block, such as letters, satirical writings and epitaphs, but here archaeological and material evidence will feature more strongly as we try to integrate different types of evidence to further our understanding of the social history of ancient Rome. You will also be introduced to some of the debates and issues raised in secondary scholarship.

3.1 House and home

> When in the past I withdrew in sadness from public affairs, my home received and soothed me; but I cannot now take refuge from domestic grief in public life, to find relief in what it offers. And so I stay away from home and Forum alike, for neither public nor private life can any longer comfort the distress which each occasions me.
>
> (Cicero, *Letters to his Friends* 250 (4.9 in Readings Book 2)

In his grief for both his daughter and the ailing republic, Cicero draws a distinction between home (*domus*) and forum. He contrasts the soothing, protective and private elements of his life at home with the public and political aspects of life in the forum. For Cicero, in the good times at least, these two elements complemented each other, each bringing their own rewards, comforts and distractions. Now in political withdrawal, Cicero is perhaps re-evaluating domestic and political boundaries.

In this section we will focus on 'house and home' and explore the extent to which there was a clear distinction in Roman life between the private and the public spheres.

Exercise

If you were writing a social history of Roman housing, what types of issues would you wish to investigate? Briefly note down the types of questions to which you would be seeking answers. Then consider what types of evidence you would use in your investigation. Do you anticipate any drawbacks or limitations in the available evidence?

Discussion

These are the types of issues and questions that I have thought of. You may have identified others or have ordered your answer differently.

- To what extent did houses reflect the social hierarchy? For example, how did the houses of the élite differ from those of the urban poor, slaves or freed slaves?

- To what extent were houses (especially of the élite) orientated towards public display rather than private use? For example, can we identify spaces used by clients, or for dinner parties?

- To what extent did houses reflect the internal hierarchies of the household? For example, did the organisation of a house reinforce the differences between master and slave, husband and wife, adults and children?

In seeking to define how the house was used and what it represented, all of the above involve elements of public and private.

In terms of evidence, you probably homed in on two main types: literature and archaeology. Literary descriptions of houses, both their physical and social organisation, would be key sources. What better way to repopulate a house than to hear some ancient voices describing who lived in it, the rooms they used and how people interacted in the domestic environment? However, as you will now be accustomed to read, the ancient voices are somewhat limited in terms of their gender, status and perspective. They do not always tell us the details that we want to hear, and the specific (generally very public) roles of the literary genres need to be remembered. Archaeology provides us with a different perspective – the remains of actual houses, aspects of their décor, such as wall paintings and mosaics, and household objects. These physical remains are a fascinating and rich source, but it is not always easy to put the people back within the walls of a derelict house and understand their behaviour.

In terms of evidence, another important aspect which may have struck you is how much actual evidence for housing survives from the city of Rome itself. When you think of Roman housing it is probably Pompeii or provincial villas that spring to mind. When visiting modern Rome, in search of ancient Rome, it is easy to identify and visit public spaces, but much less easy to see houses. Evidence for private housing in Rome is diverse – literary sources suggest the role of private housing in public life, lead pipes name house owners and many archaeological fragments survive of long-buried dwellings. Yet the private houses of Rome are 'poorly understood' (Wallace-Hadrill, 2001, p.129). Sites such as Pompeii have been very useful to studies in Roman housing, but Pompeii is very different from the Rome of our literary sources. Pompeii was a comparatively insignificant small town of traders and landowners, and many of its basic structures predated its foundation as a Roman colony.

Something else we need to keep in mind is our own modern-day assumptions about houses, their role and significance. For most of us there is a clear distinction between the private world of house and home, and public spaces – be these work, pub or gym. In general, very few people are invited into our homes, although a house, its design and décor, is often viewed as an overt status symbol. We should not assume that a Roman – especially an élite male Roman – thought of his house in the same way.

Let's begin exploring the primary evidence by addressing this issue. Can we gain any insights into how the house may have been perceived? How were people supposed to view their domestic property? We have already touched on the significance of the word *domus* in Part 2. *Domus* could mean more than just 'house' because it encompassed those who lived in the house – the household. People and relationships lay at the heart of the *domus*. The physical structure of the house was, nevertheless, of great emotional and symbolic importance. The house could unite the generations, and if it was an ancestral seat it automatically linked past, present and future. Even if it was not an ancestral home, the ancestors might still be given a symbolic presence through a display of their portraits and images. These links with the past were underlined by religion. The Lares and Penates were the guardian spirits of hearth and home, and shrines were placed within the house to which offerings were made for the well-being of its inhabitants, past and present (Figure 4.16). To violate someone's house thus had religious connotations and so the house was often perceived not only as an emotional refuge, but as a sanctuary offering protection in times of crisis.

When Cicero was exiled in 58 BCE his house on the Palatine was destroyed. This was a symbolic act: to destroy a house deliberately was to deprive its owner of an element of his identity. This was an attempt to erase

Figure 4.16
A *lararium* or
household shrine in
the House of
Menandro,
Pompeii, first
century CE. The
Archaeological
Superintendent,
Pompeii. Upon
authorisation of the
Ministry for
Cultural Heritage
and Environment.

Cicero's name and presence from the memory of his fellow citizens in
Rome. Cicero's opponents used part of the former site of the house to build
a temple to the goddess Liberty. On his return from exile Cicero addressed
the senate, demanding the restoration of his house.

Exercise

Read Cicero, *De Domo Sua* (*The Speeches*) 37.100, 41.109, 57.146–7 in
Reading 4.11.

RB

How does Cicero describe and characterise his house?

Discussion

Cicero wants his house back. However, he does not speak in terms of
the financial loss he has incurred, nor does he describe in detail what

he has lost. We gain no impression of the scale of the house, its appearance, décor or amenities. Indeed, Cicero claims not to be interested in property and 'private goods'. Instead, Cicero promotes both the religious attributes and political symbolism of the house. The site of his house has become a memorial to his humiliation; it symbolises not only his personal defeat but that of the republic. It is 'a scar on our country', which Cicero does not wish to see and which all good citizens of the republic should not tolerate. Cicero also makes much of the religious significance of the house. Note, in particular, paragraph 109 which characterises the house as a holy sanctuary. In the speech Cicero is forced to counter religion with religion. Those who destroyed his property have built a temple there, and the restoration of his house might lead to the destruction of the temple. Cicero counters this potential sacrilege by arguing that his enemies have already committed sacrilege themselves by uprooting his household gods. The house was 'built over by lawlessness masquerading as religion'.

In this speech Cicero makes it clear that his house stands for more than simply its bricks and mortar. The focus of the speech matches the demands of the context in which it was given. Cicero must paint a positive picture of himself and his actions and a negative picture of the actions of his enemies. To this end he exploits his audience's emotional and spiritual attachment to their own homes, and also associates the relationship between a man and his house with the ethos of the republic. Cicero's house is part of his identity and part of the memory he intends to leave behind him.

Cicero dwells on the symbolic importance of houses to the élite, but he does not discuss what the houses of the élite were like as places of social interaction, nor does he explore the significance of houses to other social groups.

Exercise

To gain an overview of the design of Roman houses and how they could reflect social and political status you should now read the *OCCC* entry on 'houses, Italian'.

As you read, note the types of evidence referred to.

Discussion

The entry begins by considering Etruscan predecessors to the Roman house and the importance of regular house plots on the Palatine excavated in the 1980s. The most copious evidence is noted as coming from Pompeii, but the literary source of Vitruvius is also tied to these Pompeian houses, which are in turn related to houses from Rome itself. Evidence for the imperial palaces is also noted. When it comes to housing the bulk of the population – probably in multi-storey tenement blocks – the town of Ostia (the port of Rome) is of crucial importance. So Rome provides important evidence for housing, but studies need to supplement this by using archaeological evidence from elsewhere in Italy.

You will not be surprised to read that we know more about the houses of the élite than those of other groups. This is due to literary biases, the better preservation of more substantial structures and also the tendency of previous generations of archaeologists and scholars to preserve the beautiful and the impressive rather than the mundane. However, it seems likely that the majority of the inhabitants of Rome owned no house and achieving domestic privacy would have been challenging. Slaves lived with their masters, but we have few insights into their quarters, where they slept and how they conducted their own 'family life'. Other slaves, freed slaves and free artisans lived on the job, occupying spaces above or behind shops and workshops.

Rome was also filled with blocks of flats. These would have been owned by wealthy landlords who were prepared to invest in property despite the high risks from fire and shoddy building. Rents in Rome were high and a good profit could be made. Cicero owned several blocks of flats which provided him with a steady return. Very few of these blocks of flats survive for us to evaluate their structure and organisation. One exception is a block on the present Via Giulio Romano which has four floors (Figure 4.17). The ground floor was occupied by shops with residential mezzanines, the first floor by two apartments and the second and third floors by smaller rooms. It seems likely that the higher up the building you lived the cheaper and more basic the property became. So the comparatively poor and the comparatively well off may have rented rooms in the same block. For some, free housing or assistance with rent may have been one of the perks of the patronage system; for the extremely poor there was little security of tenure with rent being collected every few days (Frier, 1980). It is easy to imagine that many of these blocks of flats were badly built and ill equipped. But in reality our knowledge is scanty and, as Purcell notes in his *OCCC* entry, 'Scholarship has concentrated on typology rather than function, and has been given to making facile assumptions about standards of comfort, convenience, and cleanliness based on modern cultural stereotypes'. Nevertheless the differences between the living conditions of the wealthy

Figure 4.17   Model of the Insula showing the whole of the right corner which now lies below the steps leading up to S. Maria in Aracoeli. Model by the architect Italo Gismondi, shown at the Mostra Augustea della Romanità in the Exhibition Building in Rome, 1937–38. Museum of Roman Civilisation, Rome. Photo: Alinari Archives–Alinari Archive, Florence.

and the poor were extreme. Just as Cicero escaped to the forum to avoid domestic turmoil, so did others. People may have been unable or unwilling to spend much time at 'home' and thus outside life and public communal spaces in Rome were of great importance.

For the élite, the house was not just of symbolic importance, but also about constructing and displaying social status. By their design and location, aristocratic houses could signify the distinction of their occupants. Such houses were typically organised around a central hall or atrium – a space where a Roman politician could meet clients and hold meetings. Traditionally, it was in the atrium that a display of the family's past might be located – wax masks of ancestors, portraits and records of magisterial achievement. Vitruvius, writing during the reign of Augustus and inspired perhaps by the latter's building projects, summed up how the physical characteristics of a house reflected the social status of its owner:

> Those rooms which no one is allowed to enter are considered 'private': bedrooms, dining-rooms, bathrooms and so on. But the public rooms are those which people have a right to go into without being invited: entrance halls, courtyards, porticoes and so on. It

follows that men of average wealth do not need wonderful entrance-halls, vestibules and courtyards, since their social obligations consist in going to pay their respects to others rather than receiving their own clients.

Those whose wealth comes from agriculture must have room to keep their livestock and produce on display in their entrance-hall; and they need cellars and granaries and storerooms and other rooms inside their houses for keeping produce rather than showing off their wealth. Similarly those who lend money and are engaged in government contracts need houses that are both pleasant and impressive, and safe from thieves. Those engaged in oratory or public speaking need larger and finer houses with room for those who come to hear them. And those of the highest status, who are involved in politics and the struggle for office and have to appear in public, must have high and impressive entrance-halls, wide courtyards and wide porticoes lined with trees to show off visibly how important they are. Furthermore their libraries and halls should be built as magnificently as public ones, since these men often need to preside over public meetings and cases requiring arbitration or legal judgements in their homes.

(Vitruvius, *On Architecture* 6, 5.1–2, in Gardner and Wiedemann (trans), 1991, p.9–10)

Vitruvius suggests that houses should be suited to their purpose. Only certain people need grand spaces, reception halls and so forth. Vitruvius is creating a blueprint for how people should design and use their houses, and thus is not necessarily reflecting actual practice. Nevertheless his description of the blurring between private and public is striking. The house is not just for the family of the élite owner. As we've seen in earlier sections of the block, its doors are often open, for guests, clients, business and for entertainment. The élite house could serve as 'the mediator between the individual and the community' (Hales, 2003, p.43).

Is it possible to look at real houses and gain further insights into how they operated? What did an atrium really look like? How accessible was it? What were the private family rooms like?

Exercise

Look at Figures 4.18, 4.19, 4.20 and 4.21.

1   Identify the atrium on the plan (Figure 4.18) and look at Figure 4.19. How is the atrium accessed? What does it give access to? What are the main features of the atrium?

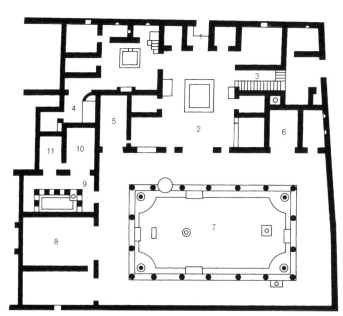

1 Vestibule
2 Atrium
3 Staircase to upper storey
4 Kitchen
5 Dining Room (*triclinium*)
6 Dining Room (*triclinium*)
7 Peristyle garden
8 Summer dining room
9 Small peristyle
10 Dining room/sitting room
11 Bedroom

Figure 4.18   Plan of the House of the Vettii, Pompeii. Taken from John Ward-Perkins and Amanda Claridge, *Pompeii AD 79*, p.49, exhibition catalogue, Royal Academy of Arts, London. Imperial Tobacco Ltd., 1976.

Figure 4.19   Atrium of the House of the Vettii, Pompeii. Photo: Alinari Archives–Alinari Archive, Florence.

Figure 4.20   Peristyle garden of the House of the Vettii, Pompeii. Photo: Werner Forman Archive/ location: 02.

Figure 4.21   Wall painting from the *triclinium* (summer dining room), House of the Vettii, Pompeii (room 8 in Figure 4.18). © 1990, Photo SCALA, Florence – courtesy of the Ministero per i Beni e Attività Culturali.

2   What other rooms are identified on the plan? How do you think these identifications were made?

Discussion

1   The atrium is marked by the number 2 on the plan. It is entered through a small, relatively narrow, vestibule. Anyone entering the house through the front door would have passed though the atrium. The atrium is an open space. At its centre is a shallow pool (*impluvium*). This was filled by rain water which entered through an opening in the roof (*compluvium*) – the latter is not visible in the photograph. A large chest can be seen to one side of the *impluvium*. A second chest is on the other side of the pool. This is not visible in the photograph, but is marked on the plan. These chests may have been used for the storage of valuable items. At the very least we can say that their placement here makes them highly visible items of furniture. The atrium gives access to other rooms, and there is a staircase to an upper floor. The peristyle garden is visible from the atrium and is accessed through it. A visitor to the house enters the atrium and is then drawn to look across the *impluvium* to the garden beyond.

2   Other rooms identified on the plan include a kitchen, a bedroom and several dining rooms. The kitchen is presumably identified as such by evidence found for the preparation and cooking of food. The plan shows the outline of an oven in the kitchen. The 'dining rooms' open onto the garden and are richly decorated, suggesting that guests might be entertained in a lavish alfresco style. But is the location of these rooms and their décor sufficient evidence to identify function? Similarly, why has room 11 been identified as a bedroom? A possible answer is because it is a small, simply decorated room, removed from the atrium and garden, and thus it has a more 'private' feel.

The house of the Vettii was not the home of a Roman senator. It did not belong to 'those of the highest status who are involved in politics' (Vitruvius). The owners may have been well to do, but they may have been freed slaves rather than part of the imperial élite. Nevertheless the house demonstrates that how we 'read' spaces is dependent on a variety of factors. What defines a room as being for a specific purpose? Its architecture, location, décor, furniture, objects and the presence of people. The houses of Pompeii provide a wealth of detail but there are many uncertainties surrounding how spaces were used and by whom. We rarely have the furniture and objects that would help us to identify how individual rooms functioned. We also need to be conscious that room use could change with time or even across the course of a day. How many of us use a spare bedroom as a study, or the dining room as a children's play area. The kitchen table is often used not just for cooking and eating, but also for studying and working. Similarly, at Pompeii, the atrium may have been designed for receiving guests, but at different times of the day children may have run around the pool. There is also evidence for partitions and curtains that might screen off parts of the house, or open up other parts of it as time and occasion demanded. The evidence may be full of caveats, but it is suggestive of flexible use. We need also to be conscious of our own cultural preconceptions about how space is used and defined. A Pompeian kitchen may not have been used just like a modern one; a room with a bed may not have equated to our idea of a bedroom; a small unlit, undecorated room at the back of the house may not have been for a slave.

In many ways what we can most readily access about houses, both through literature and archaeology, is their public side, or at least those elements aimed at public display: 'Roman domestic architecture is obsessively concerned with distinctions of social rank' (Wallace-Hadrill 1994, p.10). We yearn to know more about where the children played and the slaves slept. The use of space is governed by rules of behaviour which are culturally understood but which are not revealed in the architectural evidence. The layout of rooms does not tell us about the 'pattern of human interaction' (*OCCC*, entry 'houses, Italian', p.362). In arrangement and decoration the house advertised the power and prestige of the owner (the *paterfamilias*), and in so doing tended to conceal the presence of other inhabitants. However, we should not assume that these inhabitants were shut away or marginalised. Husbands and wives, parents and children, masters and slaves were not physically separated.

A house could say a lot about its owner. You could look back at Petronius' fictional description of Trimlachio's house and all its accoutrements in Reading 4.3 – did a freed slave, or anyone, need all this space and extravagant furnishings? And just as the opulence of dinners and tombs ('the house we live in for much longer' to quote Petronius) were often criticised – so were people's tastes in houses, décor and furnishings. Houses could be part of the moral debate about extravagant living. It could be politically expedient to make a display of modesty in how you lived. Pompey the Great, apparently, built himself quite a modest 'pad':

> When he was building the beautiful and famous theatre which is called after him, he constructed close by it, like a small boat attached to a big ship, a house for himself which was grander than the one he had before; but even this was not grand enough to excite envy. In fact, so the story goes, when the person came into possession of the house

after Pompey first entered it he was quite surprised and asked, 'Where did Pompey the Great hold his dinner parties?'

(Plutarch, 'Pompey', in Warner, 1958, pp.199–200)

An ancestral seat of a politician of the late republic who came from a distinguished ancient family might be modest by nature, reflecting the tastes of a bygone age. Indeed, in Rome, where you lived – having an address in the best neighbourhood – might be of greater significance than the nature of the house itself. During the republic, the homes of those wealthy citizens heavily involved in politics were situated near the political centre of the Forum Romanum. By the end of the republic the Palatine hill, overlooking the Forum, had become the most favoured address. In 62 BCE Cicero moved to the Palatine and in 59 BCE so did his brother Quintus (Cicero, *Letters to his Friends*. 5.6.2). Cicero's rival Clodius also owned a house here (Cicero, *Letters to Atticus* 2.4.7) (see the entry under 'Domus: M. Tullius Cicero' in Steinby, 1995, pp.202–4). The first emperor Augustus took over a number of houses on the Palatine and eventually the imperial palace occupied the entire hill. Augustus made a show of modest living – his house was to be that of a leading senator not a despot – but his successors' homes gradually became more palatial. The great fire of CE 64 destroyed the remaining republican aristocratic houses on the lower slopes of the Palatine. In the wake of the fire the emperor Nero built the ultimate palace known as the Golden House. In the imperial period there was less need for aristocratic houses to be situated at the political centre, which the emperor now dominated physically as well as politically, and thus these were spread out across the city. Pliny the Younger, for example, lived on the Esquiline, near the Porticus Livae. However, we need to remember that the extremely wealthy could own several houses and could chose to spread the display of their wealth across various venues in Rome, its environs and beyond (For examples, look up the entry for 'villa' in *OCCC*.)

Exercise

Read Pliny, *Letter* 2.17

What impression does the letter create of Pliny's villa.

Note: Appendix B of *The Letters of the Younger Pliny* (set book) is a reconstructed plan of the villa.

Discussion

One element that struck me is the importance of the forces of nature and how these had been taken into consideration in the design of the house. Note the repeated references to the weather and how the house functions at different seasons. Optimising natural light and natural resources is also important. All of these are a sign to Pliny that this is a good and well-designed house that takes full advantage of nature and the terrain – important considerations in a world without modern amenities. Overall, Pliny's villa seems large and impressive; it has numerous rooms and even its own suite of baths. Note the flexibility in purpose of some rooms, which are primarily for the use of slaves and freedmen, but are presentable enough to receive guests. Indeed, Pliny deliberately underplays any suggestion of extravagance. The 'house is large enough, but not expensive', it's convenient to get to, the area is largely self-sufficient (hence no need to import expensive luxuries) and he doesn't even fire up the furnace unnecessarily! The house is a convenient refuge from Rome – remember the contrast you encountered in *Letter* 1.9 between the busy life (*negotium*) of Rome and the peaceful leisure (*otium*) of his country villa. The house, or at least Pliny's description of it, is designed to reflect its owner. It is grand enough, but not showy; it is practical rather than extravagant; it is peaceful and private rather than loud and public. It is, however, a house in which Pliny receives guests, and thus it is still a place where he might find himself on display.

In describing his villa Pliny focuses on his own needs and his use of the space. We do gain some insights into the needs of slaves and freed slaves, but in Pliny's villa there are no children and apparently no wife. The purpose of the letter is not to describe the social activities and interactions of the villa, but to present Pliny as an owner of a refined and modest villa that provides a suitable backdrop for his élite literary pursuits (Figure 4.22). Pliny's letter is also an invitation, he is trying to entice the reader to come and stay, and thus the letter was not intended to be 'a verbal floor plan' (Henderson, 2002, p.17).

Pliny owned several houses (note, in particular, *Letter* 5.6). In these homes, Pliny, like Cicero, sought an element of privacy and retreat. Home could be a haven. Yet the privacy attained by these élite men would not have equated to the modern ideal of privacy. Remember that slaves were probably a constant presence – as *Letter* 2.17 suggests. Pliny and his wife Calpurnia may sometimes have reclined for a cosy dinner for two, but slaves and attendants would have been lingering in the background. Pliny was also conscious of the symbolic importance of these buildings. His homes reflected elements of his standing and identity, they were part of how he projected his self-image. He expected people to see his houses and to react to them (note *Letter* 1.3, in which he comments on the house of a

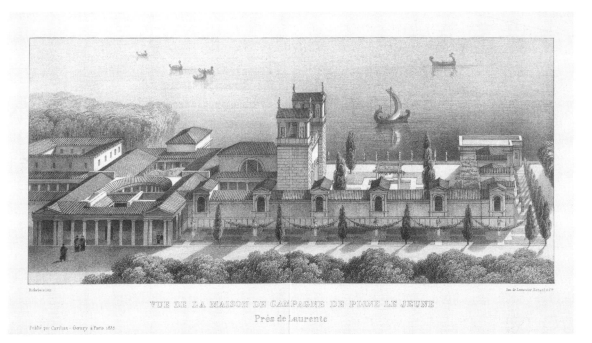

VUE DE LA MAISON DE CAMPAGNE DE PLINE LE JEUNE
Près de Laurente

Figure 4.22 *Vue de la maison de campagne de Pline le Jeune*, from Louis-Pierre Haudebourt (1788–1849), *Le Laurentin, maison de campagne de Pline le Jeune, restituée d'après la description de Pline*, Paris, 1838. Rare Books Room, Cambridge University Library. By permission of the Syndics of Cambridge University Library. A conjectured reconstruction of Pliny's Laurentine villa. Pliny's literary description, coupled with archaeological remains, has often fired the imaginations of architects and artists.

friend). Houses were not purely private places, but places to receive, entertain and impress others. The house, especially the town house, was also a place of politics and business, a locus for playing patron or client as needs demanded. In the quotation at the beginning of this section Cicero sets house and forum in opposition, but distinctions between private and public may have been easily blurred, as implied in the quotation from Vitruvius.

This section has aimed to provide a brief introduction to housing in the city of Rome, especially its symbolic and social significance. Roman housing has been an area of recent interest to Roman social historians and archaeologists, especially in terms of how domestic space was used in social terms. Scholarship has addressed issues such as room function and household activities as well as the extent to which the house reflected the social hierarchy of the household. In this section we have seen that the distinction between public and private could be fluid, for both the élite and the poor. The Roman ideal of homelife as painted in the passage quoted from Cicero at the beginning of this section may strike a chord with a modern reader, but a 'Roman' would also have had other less familiar expectations of house and home.

3.2 Theatre, amphitheatre and circus

This section focuses on the role of some of the most prominent remains of ancient Rome. Houses, of which there must have been thousands, have left few traces, but structures such as the Colosseum, the theatre of Marcellus and the Circus Maximus are among the most spectacular and evocative survivals of the city. But are these public monuments relevant in the study of social history? What can these buildings reveal about the social interaction of the city's ancient inhabitants? In this section we will consider how to set up an investigative framework for studying the social aspects of the theatre, amphitheatre and circus, and how to assess and evaluate the relevant ancient evidence. We will not set out with one question to which we are seeking an answer, but instead consider the types of questions that it might be possible to explore.

When we look at a structure such as the Colosseum, a myriad of questions can spring to mind. How was it built? Who designed it? Who built it? Who paid for it? Where did the materials come from? How was the workforce organised? When was it constructed? How long did it take to build? What other buildings were located nearby? What was it used for? How often was it used? How many people could it hold? Where and how did the audience sit? What and who could the audience see? How long did the structure last? Did the role, appearance and significance of the building change across time?

Many of these questions involve issues of social interaction. The Colosseum is about people – the people that designed it, built it, paid for it and used it. To attempt to answer all the questions listed above (and the many others that may have struck you) would be a vast project, which would involve the study of architecture, politics, economics, literature, art and so forth. Needless to say we cannot attempt to explore everything here, and nor would any sensible historian attempt to do so. Many books and articles have been written on subjects such as the architecture of amphitheatres, the historical development of amphitheatres, the political significance of mass entertainments, the content of gladiatorial shows and the lives of gladiators. The Roman theatre and circus have spawned parallel works. Thus we too need to identify a specific topic, explore the relevant evidence and establish a set of questions we wish to investigate. In this section we will continue in the guise of social historians and focus on the theatre, amphitheatre and circus as social spaces. Who used these venues? How did differing social groups interact within them?

We are starting with a broad remit but, as you work through this section, you will be encouraged to think about ways to tighten and refine the questions and issues that we are investigating. A wide subject area can often be broken down into a series of smaller areas or topics. The aim here will be to identify some of the potential topics that could be investigated rather than attempting to explore all of them in detail. In many ways this resembles what you have already been doing elsewhere in the block. It was not possible to study all the social aspects inherent in dining or slavery, so certain areas were focused on. Here you will think about some of the

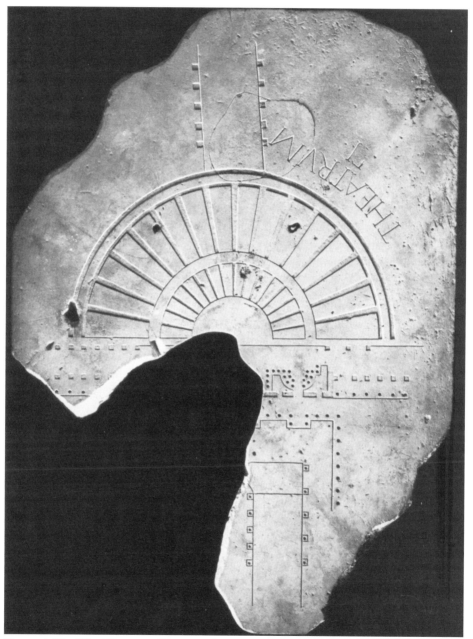

Figure 4.23   The Theatre of Pompey, Rome, shown on a marble plan dating to the reign of Septimius Severus. Photo: Fototeca Unione/AAR Photographic Archive, Rome.

choices that historians have to make: what is it possible to investigate? what types of questions can we realistically ask of the available evidence? We will need to draw on different types of evidence, and although our approach will not be primarily architectural, economic or political, these elements will impact on how we interpret the structures and their role from a social perspective.

Our raw material is the ancient evidence. This should be our starting point. What evidence is available and relevant to our topic? To what extent does the evidence shape the issues and questions that we can investigate?

Let's begin with the structures themselves (Figure 4.23).

Exercise

You should now watch DVD4, Section 2, 'Power and people: the circus, amphitheatre and theatre in Rome'. (Refer to the supporting material in Audio-Visual Notes 2 for more information.)

As you watch, think about what the surviving remains of the entertainment structures of Rome reveal about the experiences of the people who used them.

Discussion

Having watched the DVD you may well respond that the surviving remains do not tell us a lot about people's experiences! It is certainly challenging to try to recreate the experience of the original audiences and performers. However, standing outside the Colosseum one cannot but be struck by its sheer size and thus begin to imagine the impact of the architecture, scale and environment on those attending. Despite providing us with many puzzles, the buildings do evoke elements of the experience. We also gain a sense that the nature of that experience depended a lot on who you were. We cannot isolate the physical structures from the political backdrop of public benefaction and the display of power. These things seriously impacted on the interactions of those present. The gladiator in the arena, the emperor in his box, the women in the back rows – they all 'experienced' the Colosseum in differing ways. We can note, for example, how the use of separate entranceways and seats reinforced social differences. Social distinctions were woven into the very fabric of these buildings.

The structures, then, provide an evocative starting point, but we would like to know more. We need to explore other types of evidence. The DVD makes clear how literature, mosaics, sculpture and inscriptions are all integral to our understanding of the Roman theatre, amphitheatre and circus, and whets our appetite to know more. What evidence, for example, is there that supports the assertions about legislation controlling where people sat? Are there any visual depictions of an audience or crowd? Do we have literary descriptions of a 'day-out' at the races or shows? Have the entertainers left us any insights into their experiences?

Exercise

I would now like you to read Essay Nine, 'The voice of a Roman audience', in *Experiencing the Classical World*. As you read the essay evaluate:

1   the types of evidence chiefly employed in the essay;

2   the elements of the 'audiences' experience' that scholarship has focused on.

Discussion

1   The essay mainly draws on literary evidence. Other evidence – archaeological and visual – is used, but the essay suggests that it is mainly in literary descriptions that we gain insights into the ancient audience of the theatre, amphitheatre and circus. The essay notes that 'what we have comes through a filter that is predominantly male and of the wealthy élite classes' (p.195).

2   The essay tends to focus on the political dimension of the shows and on how the élite and the 'crowd' interacted. The political élite of the late republic, and subsequently the emperors, funded the shows and the structures they were held in (Figure 4.23). The audience was supposed to be impressed and entertained and thus demonstrate its gratitude and support. This political dimension intrigued some of the major authors, such as Cicero and Suetonius, who use the behaviour of the audience at shows as a barometer of the political climate and the popularity of politicians and the emperor. Inevitably scholarship has tended to focus on this element of the audience's experience since it is relatively well documented. However, the essay acknowledges that the real experience of the audience – or at least what mattered to them – may have been somewhat different. The essay notes that attendance was an experience that appealed to all the senses; that people could be passionate about gladiators, actors and charioteers and that as long as they were well

> entertained, they may not have cared greatly about the identity of the benefactors.

Although we are interested in the social aspects of the ancient amphitheatre, circus and theatre, ancient authors were often more interested in the political dimension, and this inevitably colours how the audience is defined and described in modern scholarship. We need to remember that Essay Nine chooses to highlight the relationship between benefactor and audience, and large-scale crowd dynamics. You may wish to question whether such an approach unduly prioritises some elements of these mass entertainments over others, and blurs the distinctions between the different types of shows and the impact of the venue and event on the audience. The essay does acknowledge the individuality of the experience for each audience member, but does not explore this further. In part this is because the available evidence is limited, but there are some literary sources that do capture elements of the interactions within the audience and between audience and performers.

Exercise

Many authors of all kinds mention the theatre, amphitheatre and circus, their events, spectators and performers. I would like you to read the selection listed below.

- Pliny, *Letters* 9.6

From Readings Book 2:

- Cicero's letter to M. Marius (*Letter* 30 in Reading 4.1)
- Seneca, *Letters from a Stoic* 7 (in Reading 4.5)
- Martial, *On the Spectacles* 2 and 31; *Epigrams* 5.8, 5.24 and 10.53 (in Reading 4.2)
- Juvenal, *Satires* 6 (in Reading 4.4)
- Ovid, *Amores* Book 3.2 (in Reading 4.12)
- Calpurnius Siculus, Eclogue 7 (in Reading 4.13)
- Plutarch, *Life of Sulla* 35 (in Reading 4.14)
- Suetonius, *Augustus* 44; *Titus* 8.2 (in Reading 4.15)

The types of literature represented are diverse. You have already encountered Pliny, Cicero, Seneca, Martial and Juvenal in this block. Ovid and Plutarch should be familiar from Block 3. Use the *OCCC* to find out a little about Suetonius and any of the other authors if your memory needs jogging, especially their dates and the genre in which they wrote. Remember these contextual details can be essential to how we read and interpret the evidence. Calpurnius Siculus is not listed in the *OCCC*. He is believed to have been writing during the reign of the emperor Nero (CE 54–68), but little is known of his life, background or standing. He wrote seven *Eclogues* or pastoral poems.

For this exercise I do not wish you to analyse the content of every extract in detail, but instead to think about how you might use the sources in your investigations into the theatre, amphitheatre and circus as social spaces. What do these sources reveal about people's experiences? Relevant issues to list might include insights into seating arrangements, interaction between different social groups, acceptable and unacceptable behaviour.

I suggest you use a grid to organise your answer. Make a table for yourself using the column headings shown in the example below; I've completed an entry for the first row of the table.

Author	Genre	Date	Subject	Issues
Pliny = senator	Letter	Late first century CE	Literary pursuits contrasted with the circus	Nature of the races Crowd dynamics Passionate fans Élite disdain

Discussion

My grid looks like this. You may have organised your answer differently or highlighted other issues, but I hope that you have identified some of the following.

Author	Genre	Date	Subject	Issues
Pliny = senator	Letter	Late first century CE	Literary pursuits contrasted with the circus	Nature of the races Crowd dynamics Passionate fans Élite disdain
Cicero = senator	Letter	55 BCE	Inaugural games at Pompey's theatre. The contrast between Rome (spectacle and politics) and rural life (literature and leisure)	Provision of lavish spectacles Details of performances Lack of novelty Crowd reactions Élite disdain

Seneca = senator	Philosophical letter	Mid first century CE	Adverse effects of a crowd	Crowd dynamics Inhumane impact of spectacles Moral disdain Details of combats Bloodlust of the spectators
Martial = author for the élite	Epigram (*On the Spectacles* 2)	CE 80	Titus' restoration of Rome to the people through the Colosseum	Definitions of good and bad emperors Impact of the Colosseum
Martial = author for the élite	Epigram (*On the Spectacles* 31)	CE 80	A gladiatorial contest wisely adjudicated by the emperor	Details of combat Tension and excitement in the arena Admiration for the gladiators and the emperor The novelty of the outcome
Martial = author for the élite	Satirical epigram (5.8)	Late first century CE	An attempt to thwart the seating rules	Enforcement of seating regulations Importance of appearances and being seen
Martial = author for the élite	Epigram (5.24)	Late first century CE	In praise of a gladiator	Admiration for gladiatorial skills Passionate fans
Martial = author for the élite	Epigram (10.53)	Late first century CE	Pseudo-epitaph for a charioteer	Passionate fans Brevity of life Admiration for a successful circus career
Juvenal = author for the élite	Satire	Late first century CE	Female lust for performers, especially gladiators	Range of performers Disdain for performers Performers as sex symbols

Ovid = *eques*	Elegiac poetry	Late first century BCE	Flirtation at the circus	Male–female interaction Close-packed seating Heat, dust, excitement
Calpurnius Siculus	Poetry with rural theme	Mid first century CE	A description of a show in Rome	Dazzling nature of the shows and the arena Differentiated seating Importance of appearances – being seen and seeing the emperor
Plutarch = élite Greek biographer and philosopher	Biography	Late first/ early second century CE	Sulla (138–79 BCE) meets his wife at a show	Male–female interaction Mixed seating Flirtation
Suetonius = *eques*	Biography (Augustus 44)	Early second century CE	Augustan legislation controlling seating	Seating regulations Segregation of sexes and other social groups
Suetonius = *eques*	Biography (Titus 8.2)	Early second century CE	An emperor and the people	Emperors seeking popularity An emperor as a passionate fan

The selection of texts was designed to complement the type of literary evidence chiefly explored in Essay Nine. The selection focuses on interaction within the audience, and between audience and performers, rather than overtly political evaluations of how an audience reacted to their benefactors. However, most of these authors are members of the élite, or were writing for the élite, and a political dimension is thus more subtly present. There is a frequent sense of evaluating people and their behaviour, 'people watching' rather than watching the show! The types of event that you went to see, what you enjoyed and how you behaved could be revealing. This is most apparent in the passages from Pliny, Cicero, Seneca, Plutarch and Suetonius. Others, such as Martial and Calpurnius Siculus, may appear to write from the perspective of the average man, capturing a sense of awe and excitement, but they were also writing in praise of certain emperors. So we need to be aware of the authors' agendas and potential audiences when we evaluate the sources, but this does not mean that we have to distrust all that they say.

The completed grid simplifies the material, but I hope that it enables you to see connections between the literary evidence and some of the topics and sub-questions that emerge, such as the significance of allocated seating, ambiguity towards performers and crowd dynamics. It is possible to get at some elements of the audiences' experience through literary evidence and thus complement the archaeological and architectural evidence (Figure 4.24). Ovid, for example, evokes what it was like to be at the Circus, at least in his day, and to experience the heat, dust and tension of the races even if others in the audience were not so charged with sexual tension. Other authors provide insights into how where you sat affected what you saw, how others regarded you and who you interacted with (but do note the relative dates here and how seating rules and their enforcement changed across time – an interesting topic in itself!).

2484 - ROMA - Le quattro fazioni del Circo - Museo Nazionale - Anderson

Figure 4.24 Four mosaic panels depicting the factions of the circus, early third century CE, Museo Nazionale, Rome. Photo: Alinari Archives–Anderson Archive, Florence. The panels depict charioteers next to their horses. Each man wears a differently coloured tunic representing one of the circus factions.

Let's now refine our investigation by selecting one theme and exploring this further. You may have been struck by a moral, almost puritanical view, on the spectacles and those attending them expressed by some of the authors, particularly Pliny, Cicero, Seneca and Juvenal. In the table I have identified this as 'élite' or 'moral disdain'. This is an interesting theme to explore since the attitudes of these writers have been very influential in the evaluation of the people and events they describe. In particular, Cicero and Seneca could be seen to be expressing humanity towards some of Rome's victims. A modern reader may empathise with their empathy. But is it that straightforward?

Exercise

Look again at Cicero, *Letter to M. Marius (Selected Letters* 30) (in Reading 4.1), Seneca, *Letter from a Stoic* 7 (in Reading 4.5) and Pliny, *Letter* 9.6

How and why do these authors characterise the spectacles and the reactions of the audience in the way that they do?

Discussion

These letters provide us with some insights into what it was like to be present at the theatre, amphitheatre and circus. Cicero lists the range of events – plays and beast hunts – associated with the inauguration of Pompey's theatre, while Seneca and Pliny capture the noise, enthusiasm and anger of the crowd at the amphitheatre and circus. On first reading we might see these letters as taking a rather enlightened approach to mass entertainment. You may have noted Cicero's comments about how there can be little pleasure in watching the suffering of others, and Seneca's condemnation of the mindless killing of criminals during the lunch break at gladiatorial contests. However, all three letters are written to make moral points about mass entertainment and crowd reactions. None of the authors actually condemns the spectacles and sights as morally wrong; any indignation is directed at needless extravagance in Cicero's letter, and the moral deprivations of the crowd according to Seneca and Pliny. It is not that the killings in the arena or the fickleness of the circus are wrong in themselves, but the effect on the crowd at these events can be morally damaging for the individual.

Cicero says that there was nothing new in Pompey's beast hunts and the stage plays were unexciting and performed by old actors. Cicero suggests that in the competitive environment of the late republic the audience had become saturated with novelties and was not easy to please. However, Cicero sets himself apart from the masses; he is a 'cultivated man', and perhaps the uncultivated did take pleasure in what they saw! There is also an element of irony in Cicero's account – Pompey had set out to impress Rome, and Cicero makes a play of being under-impressed in writing to a fellow intellectual who was wondering if he had missed anything. Cicero is perhaps writing with his tongue-in-cheek. For both Seneca and Pliny the crowd is simply best avoided; people are swept along by it and all too readily forget themselves. Pliny professes not to understand why serious individuals would be interested in chariot racing. Both Cicero and Pliny make it clear that they would prefer to exercise the intellect; they could indulge their chosen pleasures elsewhere, perhaps in the comfort of one of their many homes which afforded them space for leisure – a luxury that many in the crowd they so readily condemn could ill afford.

Élite authors often sought to distance themselves from the spectacles. The performers were debased and degraded and the people that enjoyed watching them were little better. The large-scale entertainments were for the masses rather than the intellectual élite; these writers would have us believe that a show was something to be tolerated rather than enjoyed. Cicero, Seneca and Pliny raise some interesting points about crowd dynamics and the exploitation and cruelty inherent in Roman entertainment. From a modern perspective, aspects of Roman entertainment are abhorrent and can be difficult to reconcile with other aspects of Roman life, and thus we may sympathise with any apparent condemnation of them. There is a danger, however, that we may read too much into their comments; after all these authors tend to condemn the crowd, not what they are watching. Think back to Part 2 where you considered Roman childhood and the points that were made in Essay Eight about projecting our own views and expectations on to the past. How far should our own cultural and moral values be used to illuminate situations and experiences that are very different from our own? You may wish to argue that some of our own experiences, although not identical to those of the ancient world, could help you to understand, or at least empathise with, elements of the ancient experience. For example, there have probably been times in all of our lives when we have been part of an audience or a crowd and may have subsumed our individual identity to that of the group. In reading Pliny's letter in particular, you may have been reminded of people's passions for football or horse racing, or for individual sports people or pop stars. But, although we may sympathise with some of the views put forward by these three writers, the perspective they take could be viewed as patronising. These authors are disparaging of the crowd and of how it reacts. The nature of the entertainments is accepted: the entertainments are not evil, but the people watching the events are. The view is one of intellectual élitism, and Pliny and Cicero, in particular, look down on their social and intellectual inferiors in a condescending manner. Admittedly, in other contexts these same authors can be more understanding. Cicero likes it when the crowd cheers for him (see Essay Nine, p.193) and it was this approval that Pompey was also seeking. Elsewhere Pliny records how a fellow writer – the historian Tacitus – was mistaken for him at the circus (*Letter* 9.23). Pliny does not condemn Tacitus for attending the races, nor is he appalled at the prospect that someone might expect him to be there. The shows were for everyone, even if some of our sources, on occasions, do not wish to be seen to be participating.

If we wanted to explore the issue of élite/moral disdain further we would need to introduce other evidence. Did others share these views? Juvenal, writing in a very different genre, also explores some of the negative influences of the shows on members of the audience (*Satire 6* in Reading 4.4). However, as we have seen, not all literary sources highlight the shortcomings of the audience. Some authors try to recreate the atmosphere in a positive fashion; they become members of the audience and capture a sense of the pleasures involved although, as noted earlier, this often entails praise of the emperor and/or the élite. Thus Calpurnius Siculus may adopt the voice of a rural peasant and try to recreate his experience and vantage point, but the purpose of the poem is to praise the emperor and his wonderful show (Reading 4.13). Literary sources, then, provide us with some conflicting perspectives. But what of other evidence? Can we gain insights into the audiences' experience, and representations of that experience, through some different types of sources?

Exercise

Look at Colour Plate 17 and Plate 46 in the Illustrations Book and read these descriptions:

Colour Plate 17 is a mosaic of Symmachius, originally from Rome and now in Madrid. The mosaic is divided into two registers intended to be read from bottom to top. In the lower register two gladiators face each other with swords raised. Male figures wearing tunics stand behind each man, and these may represent officials watching the combat. The gladiators are named: Maternus, on the left, whose name is followed by the symbol Ø indicating his death, and Habilis on the right. An inscription between the registers tells us that while the gladiators were fighting, Symmachius thrust the sword. In the upper scene, Habilis leans over the bleeding body of Maternus. To Habilis' left stands the official with his head turned towards the gladiators, but with his body turned to the left. Above him is the word *neco*, 'I kill'. Above the fallen and victorious gladiators are the words *haec videmus*, 'we see', and *Symmachi, homo felix*, 'Symmachius a happy man'. Symmachius may well have been the person providing and in charge of these games; it was his decision whether Maternus should live or die.

Plate 46 is a circus sculpture believed to be from a cemetery in Ostia, early second century CE. At the left of the relief a man and woman, in enlarged scale, are shown holding hands. The woman is of smaller stature and stands on a small base as if a statue. This may suggest that the wife had predeceased her husband. The circus scene occupies most of the panel. The charioteer is depicted twice; in a four-horse chariot, and behind this holding a palm, the symbol of victory. In front of the horses stands a figure holding a shallow bowl; this is the *sparsor* who was responsible for dampening down the race track. To his right is an individual rider. The central barrier or *spina* that ran along the centre of the circus is depicted with an obelisk, two columns bearing statues of victory and a female figure, and another group of columns for supporting the dolphins used to count laps. Triple turning posts (*metae*) are pictured at each end of the *spina*.

Now evaluate the context and form of the mosaic and sculptural relief and what they suggest about people's experiences at the amphitheatre and circus?

Discussion

The detailed mosaic shown in Colour Plate 17 is evocative of the type of scene that may have been witnessed in the Colosseum. Gladiators fight in close combat and one of them is ultimately killed. The gladiators are named, giving them individuality and suggesting the interest of the spectators in following specific fighters. As viewers we are drawn into the scene: the gladiators look at each other, the officials look at the gladiators and we look at the fight unfolding. In the upper register, the official's body is turned away from the scene, but his gaze is still on the gladiators. Perhaps he is appealing to the unseen Symmachius – who is also watching the fight. The original context of this mosaic is unknown, but it most probably decorated a floor in a house. We cannot be sure who commissioned the mosaic or who would have seen it. It may commemorate a specific games – one with which the owner of the house, maybe even Symmachius himself, was associated. The owner of house and mosaic may have been trying to relive the moment, to capture the excitement, and display it for his guests.

Plate 46 is a striking representation of the Circus Maximus. It provides insights into the appearance of the circus, especially the central barrier. The spectators were confronted not just with races but with monuments celebrating Rome's successes. The scene also captures a sense of movement and action, particularly in the strained faces of the horses. The image is compressed in terms of time and perspective. Everything appears squashed together and we see the charioteer both racing and victorious. The viewer of the relief is drawn into the excitement of the race. The relief is believed to have come from a funerary context and was probably attached to a tomb. The image of the man and woman clasping hands suggests that they were husband and wife (compare it with Figure 4.8 in Part 2). The smaller stature of the woman is suggestive of her status in relation to her husband. It may also indicate that, although her death may have inspired the commission, the memorial commemorated her husband's life, interests and identity more than hers. There is no surviving inscription to tell us exactly who was commemorated and their roles, although it seems likely that the man was connected to the circus, and may have held a position of some importance there. But we cannot dismiss the possibility that he was a passionate fan or even a charioteer. What we can say is that whoever commissioned the relief viewed the circus and its races as part of their identity at death.

As with any ancient evidence we need to be aware that these sources were produced for a specific purpose and function and had their own 'audience'. Indeed, our interpretation of these sources is hampered by the loss of important contextual details. But what we can say is that these images seek to capture certain elements of the experience for the benefactors, audience and participants at amphitheatre and circus. The original audience for these events is not depicted; instead, the viewer of the images becomes the audience. We are supposed to relive these exciting, important and expensive events. They are something to celebrate and remember. We do not know who commissioned these images or exactly how they were displayed. They may have belonged to important figures, maybe even members of the élite. But there is no disdain depicted here toward the spectators or the events. These are positive images (even if the mosaic offends modern sensibilities).

Material culture provides us with insights into how images associated with the theatre, amphitheatre and circus pervaded everyday life (Figures

4.25 and 4.26). Images of gladiators, for example, were popular and could decorate household objects. Gladiators were heroes and symbolised virtues such as courage. Arena combat was not just about death and blood. You may recall that Petronius has the fictional Trimalchio request that pictures of his favourite gladiator should adorn his tomb. Maybe for the educated élite such requests and everyday trinkets were not in the best of taste, but they underline that the entertainments were an accepted and expected part of people's lives.

Our topic of 'élite/moral disdain' has widened. We began with evidence from a handful of writers who had negative things to say about the shows and especially about the audience. We were able to contrast this

Figure 4.25 Roman terracotta lamp decorated with gladiators in combat. The British Museum, London. © The Trustees of the British Museum.

Figure 4.26   Unknown, *Thymiaterion in the Form of a Comic Actor Seated on an Altar and a Separate Theatrical Wig*, first half of first century CE, bronze with silver inlay, The J. Paul Getty Museum, Villa Collection, Malibu, California. © The J. Paul Getty Museum. This is a bronze incense burner showing a comic actor in mask and costume.

with the views of other writers who had greater empathy with the crowd. Visual evidence also provides a different perspective on audience and how spectating and 'the experience' stretched beyond the theatre, circus and arena. The negative reactions of a few can be contrasted with more positive words and images. A complex picture emerges. Some people could be critical of the shows, but their reservations were directed more at the crowd than the content of the shows themselves. Their moral concerns lay with the audience, not with the suffering of victims and performers. At times these men (Cicero, Pliny and Seneca) were part of the audience and could take positive experiences from it. Reliving that experience through, for example, mosaics and household objects appealed to a wide social mix. Among the élite there is evidence of an ambivalent attitude towards the shows: the masses were an unavoidable part of life and the shows fulfilled an important function in entertaining and uniting people of all social classes. Simultaneously, the élite did not always pretend to like the crowd or to enjoy what they enjoyed. There was a tension within the intellectual élite between wanting to belong and the fear of losing one's individuality and sense of decorum (see Essay Nine). If this ambivalence existed towards the spectators, how were the performers viewed?

To end this section let's turn to look out from the stage to the arena. To what extent can we access the performers? This could form a separate topic in itself, but it also overlaps with élite views on the shows. Questions that we could ask might include: How did the intellectual élite characterise actors, gladiators and charioteers? Can we access how these people were viewed by other members of society? And what of the performers themselves – what were their attitudes towards and experience of performing?

There is insufficient space to highlight all the evidence here, so we will just touch on some elements. A useful starting point would be the grid we drew up for the literary evidence. How were the performers characterised in these sources? You may note that gladiators, actors and charioteers could be heroes, sex symbols and inspire passionate support. They could be admired for their skills – see Martial's epigrams, in particular. But these same performers could be characterised in negative terms – they were rough and morally suspect (see the Juvenal extract, in particular). The visual evidence (which gives access to a wider social mix) also underlines their popularity, as images of performers adorned household objects and inspired rich décor. But some of these images could show degradation – scantily clad bodies, which might be bloodied and broken.

The evidence suggests that the performers – actors, charioteers and gladiators – were despised and degraded. After all, they were lowly slaves or people who had 'sold' themselves into these professions, or even criminals, who humiliated themselves and endangered their lives for the entertainment of others. The performers were infamous (*infamia* in Latin) and famous, both loved and hated. But how did the performers perceive themselves? They have left no direct voice in literature, but one source has the potential to provide some access to their life, death and self-perception – this is epitaphs on tombstones.

Exercise

Read the following epitaphs in Reading 4.8:

Charioteers:

(k) *CIL* VI 10050 (Crescens)

(l) *CIL* VI 10049 (Marcus Aurelius Polynices and Marcus Aurelius Mollicius Tatianus)

Gladiators:

(h) *CIL* VI 10190 (Superbus)

(i) *CIL* VI 10189 (Titus Flavius Incitatus)

(j) *Epigrafia anfiteatrale dell'occidente romano I Roma* N. 63 (Pardus)

What do the epitaphs reveal about the legal and social status of those named?

Discussion

The charioteers were slaves. This is implied by the single name of Crescens. The two men commemorated together are described as slaves by birth, and the father (Polynices) who commemorated them may still have been enslaved. However, both his charioteer sons appear to have gained their freedom and the names of citizens. Two of the gladiators also have single names, synonymous with slavery. However these may be 'stage names' – Pardus means panther or leopard, Superbus means brilliant or splendid. One of the gladiators is also from Egypt, suggesting that these men might be outsiders in Rome; exotic fighters would have added to the excitement for the audience. The ages at death that are recorded are relatively young. Two of the charioteers appear to have been killed on the track. The gladiators may well have been killed in the arena. These were dangerous professions! But the commemorators take pride in defining these men by their work. The charioteers' epitaphs are particularly detailed, listing victories, teams, prize money and types of races. The epitaphs list the form of the charioteers – we can perhaps imagine similar details being used in advertisements for the races. The gladiators' epitaphs are more succinct, but all give priority to the career and two list the number of appearances in the arena. There is no shame here – the men are defined as champions. The legal status of these men may be lowly and the epitaphs do not disguise this, but this is complemented by a social status constructed in terms of success and prestige.

It is unsurprising that, in the face of death, these epitaphs derive glory from the careers of the deceased. These men are defined as charioteers and gladiators – this has been their life and probable cause of death. The circus and the arena had been their home and their family. Just as slaves could form a family and pseudo-family within the *familia*, performers probably established ties within the community of arena and circus (and stage for actors). Gladiators might fight each other, but they would also perceive each other as comrades. Exploring this sense of community would be an interesting way of expanding this investigation. We could look at more epitaphs and examine further who commemorated the performers. Was it fellow performers? Were the commemorated and commemorators bound by troop and faction ties? Was it possible for these men to marry and have families? We could also look at the type of memorials involved. Were they grand or modest, decorated or undecorated? And where were gladiators, charioteers and actors buried? Did they share communal graves, were they found alongside all sectors of the community or were they buried separately? In short, could there be societies, sub-societies as it were, within Roman society?

The handful of epitaphs of charioteers and gladiators that we have looked at suggests that, although these men may not have chosen their careers, and they may not have always had their freedom, they bought into and accepted their fates (Figure 4.27). They took something positive from what, at times at least, must have been a negative experience. There is no ambivalence here, just a record of the best parts of their lives and careers. They and their commemorators view themselves as an important part of society, even if others might condemn them, their background and status. In the eagerness to be accepted and respectable the epitaphs do not provide us with a radically different perspective or voice, but they do underline that despite some élite reservations, charioteers and gladiators could secure themselves an accepted place in Roman society.

This section has sought to introduce some of the evidence that can be employed in investigating the theatre, amphitheatre and circus as social spaces. This is a broad subject and it has not been possible to explore all aspects of it in detail. Instead, the intention has been to think about ways of approaching the available evidence and how to identify topics and questions to investigate. As part of this process we looked further at one theme that emerged from the élite literary evidence, but it became clear that this needed to be placed in a broader context of other views and

Figure 4.27   A mosaic depicting a gladiatorial contest, fourth century CE, from Torre Nuova, preserved in the Borghese Gallery, Rome. Photo: Alinari Archives–Anderson Archive, Florence. Each gladiator is named, with the fallen having a crossed-through circle beneath their name.

evidence. Close reading of specific sources is an invaluable technique for the social historian (or any type of historian), but this evidence also needs to be integrated into a wider picture. What we can investigate is ultimately determined by the available evidence, its original purpose and the perspective from which it was written or produced. But as the gladiatorial epitaphs reveal, even the most humble evidence can provide us with insights into some aspects of Roman society and its interactions.

3.3   The Roman baths

The subject of this final section of Block 4 is baths and bathing in ancient Rome. The issues to be addressed here are similar to those studied elsewhere in the block, such as in the sections on slavery, dining, the family and houses. Then, as now, you needed to think carefully about the nature of the available evidence and how this could be approached and analysed. You also need to evaluate what the evidence reveals about society and its interactions. In this section we will investigate Roman bathing as a social activity. However, you will not be provided with specific questions and answers or be guided through all the material systematically. Instead, the intention is for you to practise your investigative techniques as a social historian and develop your own questions, arguments and conclusions.

Your starting point should be the primary or ancient evidence. You will find plenty of relevant material in Readings Book 2, the Illustrations Book and DVD4. I suggest you look at DVD4, Section 3, 'Roman baths' and the following plates in the Illustrations Book:

- Plate 47 (General plan of the Baths of Caracalla) and Plate 48 (Central bath block of the Baths of Caracalla)

- Plate 49 (Plan of the Forum Baths, Ostia)

- Plate 50 (Reconstruction of the Mosaic of the Athletes from the Baths of Caracalla)

- Plate 51 (Sculptural group known as the 'Farnese Bull')

See also Figures 4.28, 4.29 and 4.30.

Figure 4.28   Interior of a women's changing room (*apodyterium*) in the Stabian Baths, Pompeii, south-west view. Photo: Deutsches Archäologisches Institut, Rome/Rossa. Inst. Neg. no. 77.1924.

Figure 4.29   Bust of Asclepius, Baths of Diocletian. Museo Nazionale, Rome. Photo: Alinari Archives–Anderson Archive, Florence.

Figure 4.30   Mosaic depicting a group of bathers entering the baths. Piazza Armerina, Sicily. © Photolocate/Alamy.

For literary sources, look at:

- Pliny, *Letters* 2.8; 2.17 (esp. pp.76 and 78); 3.14; 5.6 (esp. p.141); 7.1; 9.36; 10.23 (note also 3.1, 3.5, 4.14, 7.21, 7.26, 10.32, 10.39 and 10.70)

and Readings Book 2:

- Seneca, *Letters* 56 and 86 (in Reading 4.5)
- Martial, *Epigrams* 1.23, 1.59, 2.42, 2.48, 2.70, 3.25, 3.36, 3.44, 3.51, 6.42, 6.81, 7.76, 9.75, 11.75, 12.19, 12.70 and 12.82 (in Reading 4.2)
- Petronius, *Satyricon* 26–8, 72–3 (in Reading 4.3)
- Ovid, *The Art of Love* Book 3, lines 635–41 (in Reading 4.12)
- Horace, *Satires* 1.6, lines 122–8 (Reading 4.16)
- Statius, *Silvae* 1.5 (Reading 4.17)
- Lucian, *Hippias or the Bath* 5–8 (Reading 4.18)
- Suetonius, *Titus* 8.2 (Reading 4.15)
- *Lives of the Later Caesars: Hadrian* 17.5–7 (Reading 4.19)
- Marcus Aurelius, *Meditations* 8.24 (Reading 4.20)
- Vitruvius, *On Baths* 5.10 (Reading 4.21)
- Pliny the Elder, *Natural History* 36.121 (Reading 4.22)
- Celsus, *On Medicine* 1.4 (Reading 4.23)
- Inscriptions, *CIL* XIV 98; *CIL* V 5262; *CIL* XIV 4015; *CIL* VI 16740; *CIL* VI 15258; *CIL* XIV 914; *CIL* VIII 8679; *CIL* VI 9232 (Reading 4.8 (m)–(t))

You may feel a little overwhelmed by the quantity of material, but remember this block (and the course overall) has given you plenty of experience in handling sources of various kinds. Remember to use the *OCCC* to find out about any authors with whom you are unfamiliar. Note there is no *OCCC* entry for 'Celsus'. Celsus wrote during the reign of the emperor Tiberius (CE 14–37), but little is known of his life and career and only his eight books on medicine survive. Note as well that you should not be unduly distracted by any unfamiliar names and mythological references found in the literary sources (the Statius extract, in particular). Some notes are supplied and you may, if you wish, find out more, but remember your central task here is investigating the social side to the baths and bathing.

You'll need to devise a strategy for first sifting through and then organising the material. How you do this is up to you. You may wish to begin with the archaeological and visual evidence. Alternatively you may wish to begin with literary sources, perhaps looking at the different genres (such as satire, letters, philosophy) separately, or starting with an author with whom you feel familiar (Martial, Pliny or Seneca).

However you plan to structure your initial perusal of the material I would suggest that you try to do the following:

1   initially read, look and watch as much as you can and gain a 'feel' for the available evidence and what it reveals;

2   consider the types of issues you think it might be possible to investigate;

3   work through the evidence again, making notes where you feel it necessary and identifying points relevant to your investigation.

You may find it helpful to draw up a grid like the one used for the literary sources in Section 3.2. This could easily be adapted to accommodate non-literary sources as well.

I stress again that these are only suggestions and you may wish to organise your 'reading' and initial interpretation of the sources differently. But once you have acquainted yourself with the material, you should be able to comment on the following:

•   the nature of the available evidence and its ancient context. You should be able to identify any biases created by gender, status or chronology. (Tip: remember when writing an essay that it is often a good idea to include a paragraph or a few lines addressing the issue of sources – the evidence that is available and its nature.)

•   the extent to which the evidence illuminates the social aspects of Roman bathing.

As you worked through the material you were probably struck by certain questions concerning basic facts about bathing, such as: How many people could bathe together? Did men and women use the baths at the same time? Did slaves and children attend? More complex questions may also have emerged, such as how was the social hierarchy reflected? Why did people go to baths? And to what extent can we reconstruct the social experience of the baths – was it decorous, riotous or sexually charged? In addition you may have identified certain themes or issues that run through the evidence, such as the role of benefaction, ambivalent attitudes to bathing and the baths as a locus for other activities (such as sport, eating, business, chatting and sex).

If you wanted to focus on one or some of these issues or questions, you would need to identify which sources were relevant and which were not (and why), whether any sources contradict each other (and, if so, why), or provide different perspectives (created by what? – status, gender, time?), and the extent to which it is possible to piece together a relevant and coherent impression or answer.

Apart from being familiar with the primary evidence and having some ideas as to what it is possible to investigate, it is also helpful to be aware of the state of scholarship. Roman baths have interested and continue to interest many scholars. What sort of questions have they asked? What problems have they encountered? You are working on a second-level undergraduate course, not a postgraduate thesis, and you are not expected to know all that has been written or is about to be written on Roman baths, but it helps to know what has and also what can be done with the available evidence. The *OCCC* should be a useful starting point. It is a volume written by scholars that draws on previous research. Read the *OCCC* entry on 'Baths' now.

For the purpose of this work, you may have found the *OCCC* entry a little disappointing. It is useful on the architecture of baths and to some extent on bathing as a cultural phenomenon, but apart from noting that 'bathing occupied a central position in the social life of the day' (p.115) it doesn't tell us much about the experience of bathing or its social side. This underlines a point that was made at the beginning of the block: that a social-history approach is only one way of exploring the available evidence. In scholarship much emphasis has traditionally fallen on bath architecture and engineering, rather than on the experience of the bathers. It has only been in more recent years that the various strands of evidence have been integrated to explore bathing as a social experience.

To illustrate the types of questions and issues that scholars have been exploring, Readings Book 2 contains several extracts from the following secondary sources:

- Inge Nielsen, *Thermae et Balnea* (Reading 4.25)

- Garrett G. Fagan, 'Interpreting the evidence: did slaves bathe at the baths?' (Reading 4.26)

- Natascha Zajac, 'The *thermae*: a policy of public health or personal legitimation' (Reading 4.27)

- Garrett G. Fagan, 'A visit to the baths with Martial' (Reading 4.28)

When you read these extracts you may find the following points useful:

1   *Referencing.* Remember the earlier work that you have done with secondary scholarship. In particular, look back at Block 3, Section 3.4, where you read the Wiseman journal article and considered how arguments were supported by references both to ancient sources and the work of other academics. The extracts that you have been provided with here are also supported by notes and references. At this level you are not expected to read or check all of these. The references

have largely been included for completeness so that you can see how someone has gone about researching and supporting his or her argument. To a great extent you will have to accept that these scholars have done their job well, but occasionally there may be specific points that you wish to pursue further and the dossier of primary sources with which you have been provided in Readings Book 2, the DVD and Illustrations Booklet allows some scope for this. In noting how arguments and assertions are supported by reference to the primary material, you are also provided with a model for your own TMAs. The presentation of your system of referencing may be different, but it should perform the same function of supporting your arguments, information and assertions. (See your Assignment Book for further guidance.)

2   *Context*. Scholarship, just like primary sources has a context. In general, at second level this is not something to agonise over since, for example, you are not expected to pass comment on Wiseman's or Fagan's social status, education and background in the same way that you are expected to comment on that of Pliny or Cicero. However, what you read does have an academic context. It may be particularly relevant to note the date of the things that you read. Does one piece of research predate another? How is later research shaped by what others have previously said and done? Remember how in Block 3 the assertions made by Wiseman were re-evaluated by others in the light of new evidence. You should also note where something is published and its intended audience. Is it a popular work? A journal article? A chapter from an edited volume? A chapter of a book? If so, what is the book about? Roman life in general? Bath architecture? Or bathing as a social activity?

3   *Content*. You will find it useful to make notes on the content of the extracts. What is the central argument? How is it supported? At this level of study you are not expected to critique secondary scholarship, but you may wish to ask yourself whether you find the case put forward a convincing one and, if so, why. You will also need to evaluate its relevance for the particular topic or question that you are investigating. Only some parts or points may be of importance to your own argument.

As well as reading the extracts contained in Readings Book 2, you may wish to use the internet. Please refer to the eDesktop. The internet may give you access to additional primary and/or secondary sources, but remember to evaluate what you find carefully. The Course Introduction will give you further advice.

This section has sought to introduce you to some material relevant to the study of the Roman baths, especially the social aspects of bathing. It has not been the intention to ask a single question and then find the answer. Instead, you should have developed your own questions and framework for investigation. You may well have found this challenging, but it reflects the skills that you have been practising throughout the block. These skills will stand you in good stead when you attempt your final TMA.

Part 4 Conclusion to Block 4

At the very beginning of the block you were asked to define social history and to think about how it might be studied in the Roman context. There we noted that Roman social history might be a scrappy process; that to gain access to subjects such as slavery or the family, we often need to draw together snippets of evidence from different sources, periods and places to build up a picture. At the end of the block you can now reflect on the extent to which this is true and assess the pros and cons of such an approach. On the plus side, this process can make for interesting detective work as we put the pieces of the jigsaw together in the most coherent and logical fashion. On the down side, we may sometimes create a picture that is disjointed in terms of space and time; a composite picture of Rome and 'Romans' that was never a reality.

To overcome these dangers as best we can we need constantly to ask questions of our evidence and recreate its original context in terms of space, time and role. Sometimes it is impossible to tick all these boxes – where a mosaic was found may not be known, an epitaph may have no date – but at the very least we must acknowledge that these pieces of evidence did have a specific function in the ancient world defined by their original environment.

At times social history is frustrating, not just because of the fragmentary nature of the evidence, but because the evidence just does not and cannot tell us things we wish to know. We can formulate questions to which we cannot find answers. Even when we do find answers there is often the caveat that this may only have been true for some people, some of the time. As we have seen, Pliny's Rome was not everyone's Rome. Sometimes, perhaps, we even ask the wrong questions – questions that spring from our own cultural assumptions and expectations. It can be particularly difficult for the social historian to be objective.

To list some of the negative aspects of researching Roman social history, as I have just done, can make it appear a hopeless cause. I hope that you have not found this to be the case. Yes, we need to tread carefully, but Roman social history is still fascinating and exciting. We need to be cautious of our evidence and the impressions it projects, but we need not be overly distrustful. After all, the evidence was not written, designed or made to trick us deliberately. We just need to keep a sense of perspective on the Roman views with which we are (and are not) presented.

It has not been possible to cover everything here and there are no doubt many areas about which you would like to know more. You've probably also spotted themes that have cross-cut the areas we have focused on, such as the idea of élite self-representation, or the construction of social ideals and stereotypes. Some of the topics we have focused on reoccur throughout the block. Patronage, for example, which could define relationships between friends or between ex-slaves and their masters, and could be instrumental in funding housing, tombs, shows and baths, and influence aspects of domestic and public architecture. Or dining, which could be part of the patronage system, occur at tombs or at public locations (or snacking at least) such as shows and the baths, and influence domestic architecture and décor. One subject, which has largely been left simmering beneath the surface in this block and about which it would have been interesting to have done more, is religion and its role in Roman society. The importance of religion at essential rituals – births, deaths and marriages – has been noted, but it was also significant in terms of how houses were perceived, and played an important role at public communal events and places, including the shows and the baths. Finally, you may also have been struck by connections that could be made with the rest of the course, especially the Greek world, such as the social aspects of the theatre in Athens or the portrayal of mourning and the family in the funeral speech of Pericles.

I highlight these varied themes and connections at the end of the block because they may inspire you to find out more and also because they evoke the rich tapestry of interwoven issues that contribute to our understanding of life in Rome and in the Classical World in general.

References

Basore, J.W. (ed. and trans.) (1932) *Seneca: Moral Essays*, vol.2, Cambridge, MA: Harvard University Press (Loeb Classical Library).

Bodel, J. (2000) 'Dealing with the dead: undertakers, executioners and potter's fields in ancient Rome', in V. Hope and E. Marshall (eds) *Death and Disease in the Ancient City*, London and New York: Routledge, pp.128–51.

Bodel, J. (2001) *Epigraphic Evidence: Anicent History from Inscriptions*, London and New York: Routledge.

Bradley, K. (1987) *Slaves and Masters in the Roman Empire: A Study in Social Control*, Oxford: Oxford University Press.

Bradley, K. (1994) *Slavery and Society at Rome*, Cambridge: Cambridge University Press.

Frier, B. (1980) *Landlords and Tenants in Imperial Rome*, Princeton, New Jersey: Princeton University Press.

Gardner, J. and Wiedemann, T. (eds) (1991) *The Roman Household: A Sourcebook*, London and New York: Routledge.

Grant, M. (ed. and trans.) (1956) *Tacitus: The Annals of Imperial Rome*, Harmondsworth: Penguin.

Hales, S. (2003) *The Roman House and Social Identity*, Cambridge: Cambridge University Press.

Henderson, J. (2002) *Pliny's Statue: The Letters, Self-Portrayal and Classical Art*, Exeter: University of Exeter Press.

Rawson, B. (2003) *Children and Childhood in Roman Italy*, Oxford: Oxford University Press.

Steinby, M. (ed.) (1995) *Lexicon Topographicum Urbis Rome*, vol.2, Rome: Edizioni Quasar.

Wallace-Hadrill, A. (1994) *Houses and Society in Pompeii and Herculaneum*, Princeton, New Jersey: Princeton University Press.

Wallace-Hadrill, A. (2001) 'Emperors and houses in Rome', in S. Dixon (ed.) *Childhood, Class and Kin in the Roman World*, London and New York: Routledge, pp.128–43.

Warner, R. (1958) *Fall of the Roman Republic: Six Lives by Plutarch*, Harmondsworth: Penguin.

Further reading

Beacham, R. (1999) *Spectacle Entertainments of Early Imperial Rome*, New Haven and London: Yale University Press.

Bodel, J. (2001) *Epigraphic Evidence: Anicent History from Inscriptions*, London and New York: Routledge.

Bradley, K. (1987) *Slaves and Masters in the Roman Empire: A Study in Social Control*, Oxford: Oxford University Press.

Bradley, K. (1991) *Discovering the Roman Family*, Oxford: Oxford University Press.

Bradley, K. (1994) *Slavery and Society at Rome*, Cambridge: Cambridge University Press.

Coulston, J. and Dodge, H. (eds) (2000) *Ancient Rome: The Archaeology of the Eternal City*, Oxford University School of Archaeology, Monograph 54.

Dixon, S. (1992) *The Roman Family*, Baltimore and London: John Hopkins University Press.

Fagan, G. (2002) *Bathing in Public in the Roman World*, Ann Arbor: University of Michigan Press.

Futrell, A. (2005) *Bread and Circuses: A Sourcebook on the Roman Games*, Oxford: Blackwell.

Gardner, J. and Wiedemann, T. (eds) (1991) *The Roman Household: A Sourcebook*, London and New York: Routledge.

Hales, S. (2003) *The Roman House and Social Identity*, Cambridge: Cambridge University Press.

Hope, V. (2000) 'Fighting for identity: the funerary commemoration of Italian gladiators', in A. Cooley (ed.) *The Epigraphic Landscape of Roman Italy*, Institue of Classical Studies, University of London, pp.93–113.

Potter, D.S. and Mattingly, D.J. (eds) (1999) *Life, Death and Entertainment in the Roman Empire*, Ann Arbor: The University of Michigan Press.

Rawson, B. (2003) *Children and Childhood in Roman Italy*, Oxford: Oxford University Press.

Shelton, J. (1998) *As the Roman Did: A Sourcebook in Roman Social History*, Oxford: Oxford University Press.

Treggiari, S. (2002) *Roman Social History*, London and New York: Routledge.

Wallace-Hadrill, A. (1994) *Houses and Society in Pompeii and Herculaneum*, Princeton, New Jersey: Princeton University Press.

Yegül, F. (1992) *Baths and Bathing in Classical Antiquity*, New York: MIT Press.

Zanker, P. (1998) *Pompeii. Public and Private Life*, Cambridge, MA: Harvard University Press.

Appendix   Timeline: Rome – City and People

106 BCE	Birth of Cicero
63 BCE	Cicero is consul
58 BCE	Exile of Cicero
55 BCE	Inauguration of the Theatre of Pompey
45 BCE	Death of Cicero's daughter, Tullia
43 BCE	Death of Cicero Birth of Ovid
28 BCE	Completion of Augustus' mausoleum
4 BCE	Birth of Seneca the Younger
CE 17	Death of Ovid
CE c.23	Birth of Pliny the Elder
CE c.38	Birth of Martial
CE c.45	Birth of Statius
CE 49	Seneca the Younger becomes Nero's tutor
CE 61	Birth of Pliny the Younger
CE 64	Great Fire in Rome
CE 65	Death of Seneca the Younger
CE 70	Birth of Suetonius
CE 79	Destruction of Pompeii Death of Pliny the Elder
CE 80	Inauguration of the Colosseum
CE c.96	Death of Statius
CE 100	Pliny the Younger is consul
CE c.102	Death of Martial
CE c.120	Birth of Lucian
CE c.130	Death of Suetonius
CE 216	Completion of the Baths of Caracalla